How To Whistle Like A Pro
(without driving anyone else crazy)

by David Harp

with Jason Serinus

Production, Layout, and Organization: Rita Ricketson

**Illustrated
by
Don
Mayne**

We believe that whistling is a healthy exercise for the respiratory system. But if you are currently under the care of a physician, or have any physical illnesses or disabilities, please discuss this program with your caregiver, especially the section on hyperventilation on page 34.

Printed by Spilman Printing of Sacramento, California

Dedications

Jason would like to dedicate this book to his mother, the late Mrs. Whistler; and to Dan and the late June Bell, sterling individuals and dear hearts, who have stood by him and forwarded the art of whistling for as long as he can remember; and to Lynn Davis and Kevin Ryerson, who have helped to guide his way.

David would like to dedicate this book to whistlers everywhere, from closet puckers to performing pros.

David will also partake of the same silly Whistler's Mother pun, and dedicate this book to *his* mother, Frieda Feldman; both for her early encouragement of his love of music (in the face of his pronounced lack of audible talent), and for her babysitting during the production of this book.

Acknowledgements

Special thanks to champion whistlers Milton Briggs, Marge Carlson, Jack Cohen, Ugo Conti, Bob Larson, and Roy Thoreson, for their advice, help, and musical contributions to this package.

Also thanks to: Dana and Bill Andrus (public relations directors of the 1989 International Whistle-Off at John Ascuaga's Nugget in Reno, Nevada), for their generosity in putting me in contact with the above pro whistlers; Carole Kass, President of the International Association of Whistlers; Allen de Hart, organizer of the National Whistlers Convention in Louisburg, North Carolina; whistling archivist Mitch Hider; and to everyone else who has helped this project whistle along its way!

The June Bell Whistling Fund (see Jason's dedication, above) is being established to provide a scholarship or subsidy so that a whistler lacking the necessary funds can take part in one of the national or international competitions. If you would like to make a contribution of any size, send a check made out to: The June Bell Whistling Fund, 706 Santa Susana Street, Sunnyvale, California 94086.

Table Of Contents

Part One: Foundations

Part Two: The Tools of the Trade

Table Of Contents

Introductions
David Harp

I might as well admit it now: I'm *not* a great whistler. In fact, until I began work on this, my seventeenth instructional method, I wasn't much of a whistler at all. But I am a good teacher, and good at "making simple what others have made complicated", as one of the quarter of a million people who have used my books has written to me. And I'm not embarrassed to teach subjects that I have only begun to master — my popular *Instant Flute*, *Instant Guitar*, *Three Minute Meditation* and *MetaPhysical Fitness* programs are proof of that!

Perhaps you wonder how I can teach what I barely know how to do myself. The answer is simple. I study all of the available instructional methods on a subject, and then study the masters in the field. I analyze what the existing methods and masters have in common, and what each has that is unique. I then put together a step-by-step composite instructional method, with each step clearly explained and built on the previous step.

For *How To Whistle Like A Pro*, I had to work more from scratch, since there are few existing whistle methods. So I studied some mouth physiology, speech therapy, linguistics, and acoustical physics. Then I began to: interview expert whistlers, take whistling lessons, listen to all the whistling

recordings of past and present that I could find, and offer whistling lessons to beginning and non-whistlers. Last, but hardly least, I started to whistle constantly, and to analyze why I did what I did when I did. My harmonica experience in studying the inner workings of the mysterious mouth helped me to understand the unbelievably subtle motions of the tongue and lips that the whistler must take for granted.

I combined the results of this investigation with my background in music theory and performance, psychology, and metaphysics — and you hold the results in your hand at this very moment.

The remaining element that I've added to this educational equation consists of one Jason Serinus, professional whistler. A few seconds of listening to his delightful version of Victor Herbert's *Italian Street Song* (preceding my introduction on SoundSheet #1-A) will amply demonstrate why I've included him. Jason has provided chapters on breathing, tone, and artistic expression, as well as sections that give insight into the ways of the pro whistling world. But I'll let him speak for himself, below, in italics yet!

Jason Serinus

It is with great joy that I write these words. Some years back, I had the opportunity to share some of the song that fills my heart by whistling Puccini's "O Mio Babbino Caro" as "The Voice of Woodstock" the bird in the Peanuts cartoon She's a Good Skate, Charlie Brown. *Now that David has asked me to contribute to this book, I have in addition been presented with the opportunity to share with you some of the essence of my art and technique as a whistler.*

In the early years of the International Whistle-Off (see page 78), I spent several years serving as either the "Official Entertainment" or as a judge. I remember coaching a few whistlers, two of whom credited their half hour with me with enabling them to go on to win prizes in the competition. One in particular, who later became a Grand Champion, said that the time he spent with me really transformed his art.

I did not share any great secrets with these whistlers. The essence of good whistling is not buried beneath the Great Pyramid, or locked in storerooms at the Smithsonian. It lies in your breath and in your imagination.

I have observed interest in the art of whistling grow tremendously over the last 15 years. This interest has been spurred on by such diverse phenomena as the annual International Whistle-Offs and National Whistler's Conventions, the growing Inter-

national Association of Whistlers (IAW), and the zany, campy Annual Piedmont High School Whistling Contest (regularly featured on The Tonight Show). Whistling professionals such as myself and jazz artist Ron McCroby, musicians as varied as singer Bobby McFerrin ("Don't Worry, Be Happy") and heavy metallists Guns and Roses ("Patience"), and the ever-growing presence of whistling as accompaniment for TV commercials expand awareness of our ancient art. It's great to know that after reading this book, and devoting some time to working on your own, you too will be able to whistle whatever and however you may wish.

Let me warn you about one thing. When you get to be a really good whistler, it may no longer be possible to just walk down the street whistling away anonymously. Some people will interrupt you to tell you how good you are, or to relate stories of how their grandmother used to whistle on the radio in Montana. Some may wistfully comment that they wish they could whistle "like that". Others may whistle along with your melody, or even initiate their own whistling flights of fancy. And you will begin to discover the great big whistling family that has been waiting for you to join in the making of mouth music.

Why Whistle?

As I said in my dedication, whistlers run the gamut from closet pucker-ers to fulltime professional performers and studio musicians. But beyond that, I believe that all whistlers share one common trait: they whistle because they like to. No one is forced by society to whistle, nor do people do it to elevate their social status. We do it because it feels good.

Whistling is the original joyful noise. Although, as Jason discusses in his comments on musicianship, whistling can be used as a musical vehicle to express *any* emotion, it's hard to frown while we whistle. In my recent researches, I've noticed that serious whistlers are by an overwhelming majority friendly, generous, well-balanced folk. Many non-whistlers who attend the national and international whistling events have voiced a similar observation to me.

Some psychologists have noted that the very act of smiling can raise the spirits. It is my contention that puckering has a similar effect. How can any habit that provides a means of self-expression, a way to meet people, and an instant and portable relaxation break under any circumstances not make us feel good?

Why This Book Is Named "How To Whistle Like A Pro"

No matter how skilled (or unskilled) a whistler you are right now, there are a number of elements that you will *always* want to work at improving. These are the same elements by which you will be judged in a whistling competition. The same elements that will be considered if you apply for work as a studio session "sideman", or for TV or radio commercial work. The same elements that will make (whether they know it consciously or not) your friends or passers-by enjoy your whistling, or avoid it.

These elements are clearly enumerated in the judging sheets used at the world's most popular annual whistling competition, the International Whistle-Off. They are: **Tone**, **Pitch**, **Range**, **Rhythm**, **Clarity**, **Choice of Music**, and **Embellishments (use of special effects and ornamentation)**. Although I sometimes use slightly different names for these categories than do the judges at the IWO, these very same elements are the basis of my whistling method, with a few special additions of my own. No matter how good a whistler you are, or may become, they will be your life's work. And that's why I call this book, *How To Whistle Like A Pro*.

Why "without driving anyone else crazy!"?

Like anything else — exercise, diet, study, meditation, leafblowers, car phones and positive thinking — whistling can be abused if not practiced with awareness. The habitual whistler who is unconscious of his or her effect on others can give us all a bad name with the exasperated neighbor or co-worker. One of "Dear Abby's" most responded-to columns concerned a woman's complaint about a retired neighbor who whistled continuously throughout the day (Abby recommended gratitude that it was not the sound of bickering or loud rock music).

There are two courses of action that we can take to make sure that we don't fall into the odious category of abusive whistler. We can learn to whistle well, so that our listeners enjoy what we do. And we can learn to whistle considerately, so that we remain respectful of others' auditory space. This entire book is devoted to the former, and my chapter on whistling etiquette (page 71) to the latter.

How To Use This Book

How you can best use this book will depend on who you are. Different people have differing needs, depending on how well they can already whistle. As I said on the back cover, there are two main types of people in the world:

• Those who wish they could whistle. I'll call you the pre-whistlers.

• Those who wish they could whistle *better*.

This second group can be divided down even further.

• Some of you can produce a tone but can't whistle a song. Or perhaps you can whistle part of a song or two, but not all that well. I'll call you **beginning whistlers**.

• Some of you can whistle a number of simple songs, but not so that anyone except your best friends want to hear you very often. I'll call you **intermediate whistlers**.

• Some of you can whistle many songs quite well. I'll call you **advanced whistlers**.

You may want to take a moment right now and try to figure out which category you fit into. Each of the chapters on the essential elements of whistling will be divided into beginning, intermediate, and advanced sections. But as I'll explain in the "Preview" section below, checking out most of the material in this package, beginning, intermediate, or advanced, will benefit you *no matter what* your current level of whistling expertise!

By the way: heavy duty information that I really want to emphasize will be placed in a box with a heavy border like this one, or bulleted •. Keep an eye out for boxes and bullets! Boxes with lighter borders will contain lighter material: anecdotes, whistling trivia, and other fun stuff.

Preview Of Contents

The contents of this book are divided into three parts, the first by me alone, and the middle and last parts with Jason.

Part One contains basic information that all whistlers can use, although those who can already whistle may want to skim the part specifically for pre-whistlers.

Part Two is the heart of the book: the technical skills that make a good whistler.

Part Three contains material that didn't quite seem to fit into Parts One or Two, but still felt important (or fun) to include. I'll go into more detail, below.

Part One: Foundations

Yes, it's basic stuff. Some of it may seem obvious. But even if you think you know your mouth, your music theory, and your rhythms — understanding the particular terms that I use and the ways that I think about these subjects will help you to use the rest of the method. And if this is not yet familiar ground — it should and will be!

The Exploration Of The Mouth

I'll begin the book with an exploration of the mouth. Whistler and would-be whistler alike should use this section, so that we can agree on the names of places that lurk deep in the constantly used but rarely investigated oral cavity. You'll learn that you have muscles in places where you didn't even know you had places!

For Pre-Whistlers Only

I'll provide help for pre-whistlers, spending some pages in the book and minutes on the recording teaching you to get that first faint whistle out. It's not easy. But while you're working on that (which can take anywhere from a few minutes to a few days or even weeks), you can continue to read and listen to the rest of the method, which will amuse, educate, and prepare you to be able to whistle better, once you can whistle!

Special Note For Advanced And Intermediate Whistlers

Please check out the following two chapters. Although they are placed way back in Part One with the pre-whistling material, I believe that even the most accomplished whistlers will benefit from a quick review of the basic building blocks of music. And you less practiced or beginning whistlers will use them to create a sturdy foundation for a lifetime of high-rising sound!

Music Theory For The "Musically Insecure"

You don't need to know about sound or music theory to make music. But it sure helps. This section is an entertaining and painless look at why sound behaves the way it does, and at why music is the way it is. You'll leave it with a clear understanding of chromatic, major, minor, and blues scales — on which virtually all of the music of our culture is based.

We've Got Rhythm

Some people are born toe-tappers, for others it's a learned skill. Whichever category you fall into, these rhythm exercises will help you co-ordinate toes and tongue!

Part Two: The Tools Of The Trade

I was initially tempted to divide Part Two of the program up by *level*, into one chapter each for beginner, intermediate, and advanced whistlers. But the more I worked with whistlers of varying skill levels, the more I realized that someone might have pretty good breathing habits, but not much understanding of how to produce good tone and tonal effects. Someone else might have good tone, but a distinctly underdeveloped sense of pitch (the highness or lowness of a sound).

So I decided to divide Part Two up by *subject*, including chapters on breathing, pitch, and tone and tonal techniques. Of course, there is some overlap, so even if you are more interested in some subjects than others, you'd better read about them all!

For each subject I'll present a *range* of instruction, from beginning to advanced level. You can read the entire chapter and listen to the recording, then go back and work on as much as seems comfortable right now. Or you can go from the beginning section of one chapter to the beginning section of the next, then do all the intermediate sections, and then all the advanced ones. But I would generally suggest at least skimming all of the information in each chapter. Then, as you work on what you can handle today, you'll know what you're striving towards for tomorrow as well.

On Breathing

Obviously we all need to breathe, virtuoso and beginner alike. This section will provide advice and exercises from Jason and me on how to improve your whistling by concentrating on the respiratory process. Most of the instruction will be of use to any level of whistler, so everyone should read this part of the book, and begin to breathe better!

On Pitch

The Harvard Dictionary of Music defines the word pitch as "A term referring to the high-low quality of a musical sound." So pitch, for whistlers, usually means the ability to whistle a particular sound at will. But my section on pitch goes way beyond that, to include training of the ear, the tongue, and the mind. I'll train your ear to hear the different notes of the most often used scales, and train your tongue and lips to whistle those notes. I'll also help you learn how to use both music theory and your sense of pitch to perform existing songs and to create improvisations of your own.

Your Whistling Range

Now that you understand the concepts of key, note, and octave (you *did* read and listen to the music theory section, I hope), you can apply your knowledge, and begin to figure out just how high and how low you can whistle. Then you can work on increasing that range. You'll also learn to figure out how to start a song on the note that will best fit your particular range, and how to "jump octaves" to accommodate songs beyond your current range.

On Tone

At the beginner level, the "tone" section will help you to produce clear and pleasant sounding whistle notes. But as you progress to the intermediate and advanced levels, this section will provide you with the special effects that separate the merely good whistler from the great one. Vibratos, trills, and warbles will be described and illustrated, simply at first, then in more and more complex combinations — until you can identify and even mimic their usage in the recordings from the world's best whistlers on SoundSheet # 2!

Part Three: The Rest

The title says it all – information that didn't fit elsewhere but that I couldn't bear to leave out.

Musicianship

In this section Jason and I will discuss the emotional range of the whistler, how to select songs for your repertoire, how to put both your head and your heart into your music, and much more. We firmly believe that with a bit of musicianship and a lot of feeling, even a beginning whistler with limited technical skills can produce pleasing music.

Pro Tips

Here Jason and I will cover warming up, microphone and monitoring techniques, and the "use" (yes, use) of stage fright.

Zen And The Art Of Whistling

With music, as with most creative arts, much of the process is beneath the reach of the day-to-day consciousness. This chapter can help you to utilize subconscious resources in your whistling. It may be beneficial to read this one early on.

Jason Serinus: The Whistling Voice Of Woodstock

Yes, it's the story we've all been waiting for — the tale of how Jason became the voice of America's best-known bird — Snoopy's friend Woodstock in "You're A Good Skate, Charlie Brown".

The Champions

The whistlers featured on the recording are some of the world's best. Featured are the 1979, 1980, 1984, 1985, 1986, and 1988 Grand Champions of the International Whistle-Off. I'll provide pictures and biographical information about the whistlers, technical information about their works featured here, and purchasing information on their other recordings.

The Competitions: The International Whistle-Off And The National Whistler's Convention

The International Association Of Whistlers (IAW)

Teaching Kids To Whistle

This section is just what it sounds like. We'll help you to use the material in the rest of the package to teach children how to whistle. The younger you are, the easier it is to learn!

That's It, Folks!

Yep, that's the preview. Enough talk. Now it's time to actually use the method!

About The Recorded Sections

I believe that it's silly to try to teach music by just writing about it. Usually I include a 90 minute tape cassette with my music instructional methods (which you can read about in my Sales Pitch on page 80). But my distributors wanted me to try doing a lower cost book with a flexible recording known as a "SoundSheet" bound right into the spine. I just couldn't restrict myself to the maximum of sixteen and a half minutes that they had in mind, so I've included *two* SoundSheets for a total of 33 minutes recording time.

I'll refer to them as SoundSheets # 1 and #2, each with an "A" side and a "B" side. I'll place a small SoundSheet logo in the book whenever a section is demonstrated on the Sound-Sheet. It looks like this.

Since I'm used to having 90 minutes in which to demonstrate and pontificate, 33 minutes didn't seem like much. So I avoided dividing the sides into the "cuts" that you'd find on a regular record, since each cut reduces the total usable time by 20 seconds. I also didn't put much of my own whistling on the SoundSheets. Although I've improved daily since beginning this book, I still preferred to use the audio time to present instruction and the champs, rather than to showcase my own limited skills.

The SoundSheets are supposed to last for hundreds of replays. But if you really want to use them effectively, please record them onto a cassette. Write down where each section of the book can be found on the cassette (in the book or on the cassette label), by using the counter on your deck. This will make it easier if you want to listen to just a few seconds worth of recording over and over again. And you will!

A Few Words About Tone Deafness

No one is.

I've worked with many hundreds of students (in person, tens of thousands more through my books) who thought they were tone deaf. None of them were. If you can hear, you can make music. Here's a little demonstration. Can you hear the difference between these two sentences?

• "That's our hotel." (What you tell the cabdriver when you near your stop)

• "That's our *hotel?*" (what you say to your friend on seeing the incredible dump where he has made reservations for your vacation stay)

In the second sentence, the tone of the speaker's last syllable has gone up. You may have never realized that this is how we indicate a question mark when speaking,

but you've recognized it all your life.

Similarly, you may never have understood music theory. You may never have been able to play a musical instrument. You may never have gained the control over your voice (or your whistle) that would allow you to reproduce songs accurately. But if you can hear, you're not tone deaf. And if you can believe me enough to suspend your skepticism, and make a sincere and diligent attempt at using this package, I'll prove it to you.

Part One: Foundations

For Everyone: Exploration Of The Mouth

Much of the work of whistling is done by the tongue. I've learned a lot about tongues in my twenty years of harmonica playing, and one of the first things that I learned was that I had never learned much about my tongue. So in the interests of reducing our lingual ignorance, let's take a quick trip through our mouths, using our tongue as a sort of of exploratory tool. We'll see if we can learn to identify structures by how they feel, even if they lurk far from the light of day. This will help us agree on the terms that I'll be using to describe tongue position during whistling.

• Begin by touching the back side of your lower front teeth with the tip of your tongue. That's it, do it right now. Un-huhhh.

• Locate the place at the bottom of your lower front teeth where they meet the gums.

• Keep moving the tip of your tongue down, into the "trough" at the very front of the bottom of your mouth.

• Continue even further down and back in your mouth. Can you feel the membrane that connects your tongue to the bottom of your mouth?

• Now touch the back side of your upper front teeth with the tip of your tongue.

• Reach up a fraction of an inch, and feel the place where your upper front teeth meet the gums.

• Continue back along the roof of your mouth for another fraction of an inch, until you feel the hard ridges.

• Keep going back until the roof of your mouth becomes hard and smooth. This is your hard palate. What does it feel like there? The bottom of a boat, maybe?

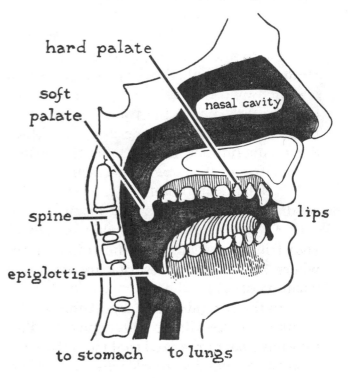

• Continue even further back until the roof of your mouth becomes slightly softer. This is the soft palate. Touching it with your tongue may tickle, or even trigger your gag reflex.

• Place the tip of your tongue on the upper surface of your left rearmost bottom molar. Touch the upper surface of each tooth until you reach your right rearmost bottom molar. Go back from right to left along your toothtops, and count each tooth with your tongue. Does the top of each tooth feel different? Some are flat, others sharp. others in-between...

• Do the same thing with the bottom surfaces of your upper molars, from left to right, then back again from right to left.

• Now use your tongue tip to identify the right side of the bottom surface of your left-hand upper molars (that's the side closest to your tongue). Read that over again if you need to. Do it again.

• Use your tongue tip to identify the left side of the bottom surface of your right-hand upper molars (that's also the side closest to your tongue). Do it again.

• This is an important one. First, do the last two exercises once more. Now flatten your tongue (as though you were saying "oyyy") so that you can feel the right side of the bottom surface of your left-hand upper molars with the upper rear left side of your tongue, and so you can feel the left side of the bottom surface of your right-hand upper molars with the upper rear right side of your tongue. Confused? See right. Do the two previous exercises a few more times. It's important, because your tongue will often be in this position when you whistle.

• For your last exercise, hump up the middle part of your tongue to scratch the roof of your mouth, as though your hard palate itched at dinner and you were too polite to scratch it with your finger.

• Now go back and see if you can do all of these exercises while you hold your lips in the position that you would use when trying to blow out the candles on your birthday cake.

Just for variety, let's do some lip and cheek exercises. Say "poo" with your lips held in close to your front teeth. Now say "poo" with your lips held normally. Now say it with your lips pursed way out, as though you were amusing a baby by pretending to reach out your lips to kiss it on the nose. This last position is sometimes known by the technical name of the "fishface" or "fish-lips".

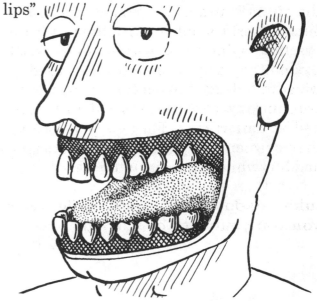

Check out your cheeks by making a few "pah" sounds, first with your cheeks held tightly in, so that the insides of your cheeks are against your teeth, and then allowing your cheeks to puff out as much as they like while you "pah".

Take some time, and play with your tongue. It's a fascinating muscle, rather more like the trunk of an elephant than an arm or leg, since it is composed of ten different muscles. Six are internal muscles, connected only to each other; and four are external muscles, that anchor the tongue to various parts of the mouth. These muscles allow us to move the tip and sides and middle of the tongue independently. So see what you can do with it. Do some tongue work at a boring meeting, or on the bus, since no one can see what you're doing!

Articulation

Using the tongue and lips to break up the air as it passes from the lungs to the outside world is called articulation. Please practice saying these words. Nonsensical though they may seem, all will be used in whistling effects (I'm really *not* just making cruel fun at your expense with these tongue and lip contortions). For now, just observe the movement and placement of your tongue and lips while you articulate.

tuka dada ladle loo oodle you you-you-you-you oy oy-you

The Pre-Whistling Stage:

Encouragement

I won't lie. Learning to whistle as an adult can be pretty tough. With this said, it's time for some *en*couraging words.

As you may have noticed while performing the articulation exercises, you can already do a great number of amazingly subtle things with your mouth. For instance, say "suh", and then "shuh". Say "dah", and then "tah". It's tremendously complicated, even for speech physiologists, to analyze and describe the difference between the first pair, and almost impossible between the  second. Yet you learned to do it as a child, and perform it and similar miracles hundreds of times a day, never even thinking about it.

Were you to try to learn to differentiate between forming "dah" and "tah" now, it would be immensely hard, rather like learning as an adult to roll the "Spanish R" for the first time. Yet millions of Latin American toddlers do it effortlessly.

Whistling is similar. Learned as a child, it seems natural. If you've never done it before, it's going to take some practice and experimentation until you hit the exact tongue and lip configuration that produces the whistle.

A New Muscle To Play With

As one last piece of encouragement, I'd like to teach you to recognize and even use a muscle that you probably don't know you have. Stand in front of a mirror, and open wide. If you really want to see what's going on in there, shine a flashlight at the very back of your throat while you do this.

Breathe normally, with your tongue lying relaxed in your mouth, or slightly extended. Notice that if you want to breathe through your nose only, you must raise the back of your tongue to block the air from passing through your throat.

Now here's the exciting part. Breathe normally again, without making any attempt to avoid breathing through your nose. Suddenly change to breathing through your mouth only, as though you were preparing to cough or blow out. You will see your soft palate (with its dangling "uvula") rise and move to the rear of your mouth to block off your nasal cavity, and thus prevent passage of air through your nose. Saying "gung" will have a similar, if less pronounced, effect.

Always keep your nose closed off when whistling. You may open your nose to help you take a quiet breath. But you *must* keep your soft palate raised (to close the nose) when you whistle or try to whistle.

Tongue Fun

Now is a good time to observe your tongue in its natural habitat. Say all of your articulations. Try a "ging", and see the middle part rise in the back. Make it short and fat, all piled up in the rear of your mouth. Extend the tip way out, curl it back and over, or down and under.

• Here's an important whistling position: flatten the back of the tongue, pushing the sides up against your upper molars. Now, with its back still flattened and raised against the molars, move the tip alone up and down. (See picture, page 16.)

The Three P's: Preparation, Position, And Practice

You've already done most of the preparation. Now it's time to look for the right position, and then practice, practice, and practice.

Everybody's mouth is a bit different, so the tongue and lip positions required for the supersubtle act of whistling can be hard to identify. The positions necessary to produce vowels, for instance, are quite standardized. Nearly everyone will produce an "ee" sound if they move their tongue high and far forward while spreading their lips widely and exhaling (while allowing the vocal chords to vibrate). Nearly everyone will produce an "oo" sound if they keep their tongue raised in back, but also move the entire tongue as far down in the mouth as possible while exhaling through a round lip hole.

But, unfortunately, whistling mouth positions are far more exacting than "ee" or "oo". It's possible to produce "ee" or "oo" with a variety of tongue positions. Whistle position is more demanding, more like the difference between the "dah" and the "tah", hard to even describe...

Suggestions On Tongue And Lip Position

Generally, here are some hints, with the most crucial ones double-bulleted. (try not to be intimidated):

•• nose must be closed off!

• Upper and lower teeth should be between 1/4 and 1/2 inch apart

• lower lip should probably be less far out than upper lip

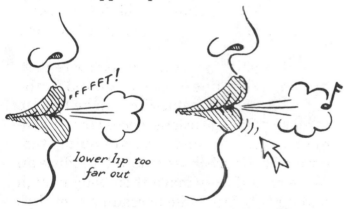

lower lip too far out

• lower lip is held slightly out from lower front teeth

•• the lip opening should be fairly round, rather than oval-shaped

•• there should be a "V" shape in the lower lip (this helps to create the roundish hole)

• there probably will be a slightly crimped feeling in middle of the lower lip, and the filtrum (muscle between nose and mouth) thrusts out slightly

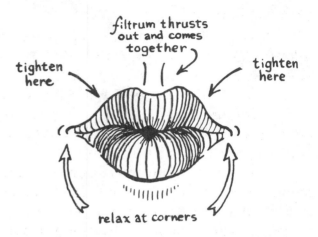

filtrum thrusts out and comes together

tighten here

tighten here

relax at corners

• "oo" or "poo" is a very vague approximation of the lip position

• lips neither too dry or too moist

•• the sides of the top of the tongue must be touching bottom or inside edges of upper molars on both sides (so that a flat air channel is left open)

• other than the above, the position of the tongue depends on the note that will be produced

for lower tones, the tongue will be further down and back (like "oo")

for higher tones, the tongue will be further forward and up (like "ee")

• lips will probably be slightly tighter for higher notes, and looser for lower ones

Some Additional Hints

• Check out your lip and tongue position with a mirror, as you review the pictures in the section and the above position suggestions.

• Experiment with changing the volume of air that you're using. Try more, or try less. Generally, enough air so that you can barely feel it on your hand from ten inches away is a good level to start with. But vary it, up and down.

• Try beginning your air flow with a hint of a cough.

Common Problems

• A hissy sound often indicates the front or middle of the tongue being too close to the roof of the mouth.

• Hissing may also indicate that the upper and lower teeth are too close together.

The Two Clutch Analogies

"How", you are probably saying, "can I possibly keep all of that in mind at one time?" It's rather like learning to drive in a car without an automatic transmission. At first, trying to learn to control the clutch pedal, the brake pedal, and the gas pedal all

at once while learning the gearshift lever positions and steering with the wheel and observing traffic laws and watching for pedestrians and listening to the driving instructor may seem overwhelming. Eventually it becomes second nature. You can talk and eat a sandwich and look for your favorite tune on the radio while driving merrily along.

There's an even more specific analogy here. Looking for the combination of lip and tongue position that will produce your first whistle is like getting into a strange car. You need to gently release the clutch, while looking for a hint of the point at which the car will begin to pull forward. At the same time you need to give it a bit of gas, not too much or too little. Think of the clutch pedal as your lip and tongue position, and the gas as your breath volume. No, it's not an easy thing to do.

The Bottle Analogy

Find a medium-sized bottle (I prefer a 12 ounce beer or soda bottle) and blow across its mouth. Listen carefully. Study and adjust the relationship of your lips to the bottle to get first any sound, and then the deepest, richest sound that you can obtain. Now fill your bottle partway with water to raise the sound. Does that change the lip position you need to use?

The actual lip and tongue positions used in making a bottle sound have little to do with whistling positions. But the *process*

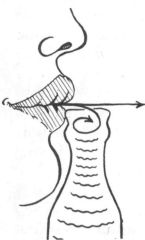

is similar. Both require sensitivity, a willingness to experiment, and the ability to listen for that first faint sound while being aware of the mouth position used to produce it. And once that first sound occurs, it is simply a matter of further adjustment and experimentation, to hone and refine and familiarize yourself with the technique.

Listening For The First Faint Signs

Practice while you do anything — while you study, or cook, or walk the dog. It could take many hours of work, but eventually, by following the zillions of instructions above, you will get a quarter-second's worth of faintly whistle-like sound. Once you do, you know that your lip and tongue positions are "in the right ball park".

How To Whistle Like A Pro!

1-A

So work on getting your whistle, but meanwhile continue on in the book and listen to the recording. Even if you don't get enough of a sound to use with the exercises, many of them can be done without whistling. And try not to get discouraged. Remember the *other* three p's: persistence, patience, and more practice.

If you do find yourself getting discouraged, please try to be compassionate with yourself. Learning to whistle as an adult isn't easy. In fact, many of the whistlers with whom I've talked claim that it isn't possible to teach someone (other than a child) who has never done it. Of course, while they are champion whistlers, *I'm* a teacher. And I *have* taught "virgin" adults to whistle. It has been difficult. Need some consolation? Check out the Breathing Meditation on page 38. It's worth more than all the rest of this book put together. And I guarantee that you can do it, today!

Raspberries

Chris von Rosen learned to whistle at the age of four, while picking raspberries with her older brother and sister. Since more of Chris' berries were ending up in her mouth than in her basket, her brother made her sing while picking. But she soon learned to sing and eat simultaneously, so he taught her to whistle. She never learned to eat and whistle at the same time, but she gained a lifelong hobby!

Music Theory For The "Musically Insecure"

You might call this chapter "everything you always wanted to know about music but were afraid to ask". It's a simplified overview of the physics of sound, and the history and theory of music.

If this chapter seems like *more* than you wanted to know about sound and music, just read the boxed summaries and listen to the recorded section on Sound-Sheet #1-A. You can come back to the rest, later.

Good Vibrations

Imagine a bumblebee that has suffered the indignity of falling into a swimming pool. Its wings vibrate, and these vibrations make tiny waves in the water. These waves make a leaf near the edge of the pool vibrate at the same speed as the bee's wings are vibrating.

Whenever *anything* vibrates, it creates additional vibrations that spread through the air. Sometimes what is vibrating is obvious, like the head of a drum or the wings of a mosquito or a guitar string.

Sometimes what vibrates is not so obvious, like the column of air which vibrates inside a flute or the bottle that we blow into. Blowing across the hole of the flute or the mouth of the bottle sets up complex air currents when the air hits the edge of the hole. Some air goes in, some bounces back out. These air currents make the air inside the flute or bottle start to vibrate. The vibrations then spread to the air outside.

The speed of any of these vibrations will vary, depending on

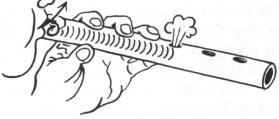

what is vibrating. The drum head vibrates at a low speed, and sends big, slow waves through the air. The mosquito's wings vibrate at a very high speed, and send tiny, fast waves through the air. The vibratory speed of the flute or the bottle's air column will depend on the amount of air that is inside to vibrate.

In the flute, the longer that the vibrating column of air is (the more holes that are closed off by fingers), the more air vibrates inside the flute, and the more air there is to vibrate, the slower the speed of vibration. Same thing with the bottle. The more open space there is inside, the more air there is to vibrate, and the slower it vibrates. Put some water inside, and there's less air to vibrate, so the air vibrates faster.

Air, Ear, And Brain

When vibrations in the air reach our eardrums, our eardrums then vibrate at the same speed as as whatever is vibrating, just like the bee's wings made the leaf vibrate.

A complicated set of bones, organs, and nerves connect our eardrums to the brain. They convey messages which let the brain know how fast the eardrums are vibrating. When our eardrums are vibrating slowly, our brain interprets this message as what we call a low sound. When our eardrums are vibrating quickly, our brain interprets this message as what we call a high sound. Thus hearing is an interaction taking place amongst the air, the ear, and the brain.

How Your Whistle Works

To be quite honest, I'm not sure. It is something like a flute or a bottle, in that air blown across the edge of a hole causes a confined chunk of air (the air inside your mouth) to vibrate. Some of the physics books that I've read say that the air of the whistle is divided by the edge of the teeth — but if I cover my teeth with chewing gum, I can still whistle pretty well. So I believe that the "edge" may be formed by our lips.

We can easily feel that some of the air blown through our pucker goes straight through, and some swirls and eddies around inside our mouth, vibrating the inside of our cheeks.

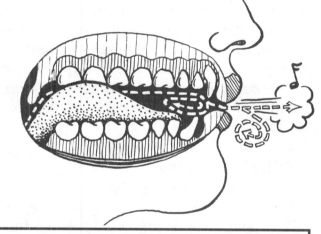

In any event — just like with the flute or the bottle — when we whistle, the size of the open space in our mouth determines the amount of air that can vibrate. The amount of air that can vibrate determines the speed of the vibrations produced. The less open space, the higher the speed of vibration, and the higher the sound. The more open space, the lower the speed of vibration and the lower the sound.

Octave Notes

Please consider any particular vibrational speed which produces a sound, like 200 vibrations per second (vps), for example.

If we compare this particular sound, (which can also be called a **note**) with the note produced by 400 vps (exactly twice as fast), we'll find that the two sounds seem remarkable alike, although the faster vibration sound is obviously higher. If we double the speed of vibration once again (800 vps), we find that all three sounds (200 vps, 400 vps and 800 vps) bear a great similarity to each other. Likewise the sounds produced by 300 vps, 600 vps and 1200 vps sound alike, and so on. Doubling the speed of vibration of a particular sound will always produce a new sound that seems to repeat the sound quality of the first one, only higher. We call these similar notes **octave** notes. We can also call the distance between two of these octave notes **one octave**.

Most people can immediately hear the similarity of these octave notes. Please listen to my demonstration of octave notes on the recording.

Pythagoras

2500 years ago the Greek metaphysician Pythagoras turned his brilliant mind to the question of why a bow string produces different sounds when stretched to different degrees. He soon discovered that lengths of string stretched between two points with equal tension would produce varying sounds depending on the length of the string.

Pythagoras began to experiment with the sounds produced by plucking different lengths of string. He noticed that if he plucked two strings simultaneously when

one was exactly half as long as the other, they would both produce sounds that somehow seemed very similar, even though the shorter string made a sound that was clearly higher.

Modern musicians now know that the "half-as-long" string was vibrating exactly twice as fast as the longer string, and thus the shorter string was producing an octave note which sounded very much like the longer string's original note. But the vibrational nature of sound was not discovered until nearly 1700 A.D., so Pythagoras had only the relative lengths of the strings to base his research on.

The Ancient Greeks And Their Ratios

The ancient Greeks were heavily into ratios. They used them in their mathematics, in their architecture, and in their art. For example, the ratio of a male statue's neck to its wrist was always 2 to 1, and the ratio of the height of the head to the length of the body was 7 to 1. So it was natural for Pythagoras to want to apply ratios to his musical musings.

He reasoned that if the

mathematical ratio of 2 to 1 (one string twice as long as the other) would produce two sounds that seemed so similar, perhaps other simple ratios like 3 to 2 or 4 to 3 could be applied to the lengths of vibrating strings to produce more sounds that somehow "related well" to each other.

The Chromatic Scale

Pythagoras continued his experimentation. He used a variety of mathematical ratios (like 5 to 4, 3 to 2, 4 to 3, etc.) to divide up the musical distance between two octave notes into smaller sections. Eventually he ended up by dividing each octave into 12 equal sections.

We call this process of breaking up the octave distance into a number of smaller pieces "creating a scale". The word **scale** refers to a particular way of dividing that octave distance into pieces. Pythagoras' 12 note division (actually a 13 note division if you count the first and last note of the scale, which are really the "same" notes, one octave apart) is still the basic scale used by most of our Western civilization's music and musical instruments. It is called the **chromatic scale**.

You can begin a chromatic scale on any note, and just play up thirteen black and white notes (including the beginning and ending notes). After I've told you about note names, I'll give you two examples of chromatic scales, marked off by the upper and lower brackets in the picture below.

Why did Pythagoras do it just this way? No one today knows for sure, but a quick look at the piano keyboard (which usually contains seven and one third chromatic scales next to each other) will clearly show that Pythagoras' 12 note octave division, has stood the test of time!

The Letter Names Of Notes

By the late middle ages each piano note had been assigned a letter name. The white notes are indicated by a simple letter (C - D - E - F - G - A - B - C), but each black note has two names.

One letter name is called a **sharp** name. Sharp means "higher than". The sharp name tells us which white key the black key is a little bit higher than. So the black key named "A sharp" is the black key a little bit higher than A. Sometimes instead of "sharp", we use the symbol #.

Chromatic Scales On The Keyboard

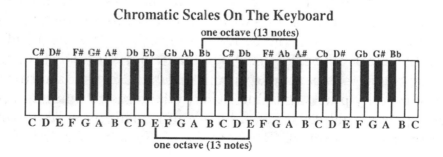

The other letter name is called a **flat** name. Flat means "lower than". The flat name tells us which white key the black key is a little bit lower than. So the black key named "B flat" is the black key a little bit lower than B. Sometimes instead of the word "flat", we use the symbol b.

You can see that A sharp and B flat are exactly the same note. Please look at the picture of a piano with all the letter names for white and black notes (both # and b).

When we choose a note to begin a scale on, the name of that beginning note is then the **key** of that scale. This will be important to us later on when we begin to learn our "range", so that we can tell other musicians what scale (or key) we like to whistle in.

Solmization (DO RE MI) Note Names

Since we're not piano players, with lots of notes to look at, another way of naming notes, called **solmization**, may be more useful for our purposes. In solmization, each note of the chromatic scale is given a syllable name, like this.

DO di RE ri ME FA fi SO si LA li TI DO

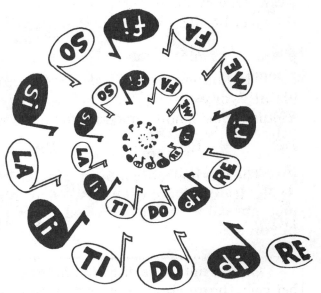

Solmi names are not as specific as letter names, but they do accurately describe the *relationship* between notes. A di is always one note up from a DO on the piano for instance, and a si always six up from a RE (counting black and white keys as exactly the same). Thus both the E chromatic scale that I played for you and the Bb one are called by the same solmi names.

All DO notes are exactly one octave apart, and sound very similar to each other. All RE notes are one octave apart, and every RE sounds similar to every other RE. This picture may help to illustrate for you the repeated nature of the chromatic scale.

The Major Scale, the Minor Scale, and the Blues Scale

Many different types of scales exist, and each scale is used to create a different kind of music. In a way, we might consider a scale to be a kind of "musical alphabet". By using various combinations of the 26 letters of the English alphabet we create English words, sentences, paragraphs and books. By using the letters of the Russian alphabet we create

Russian words, sentences and long dreary novels. Likewise, the notes of any particular culture's scale, be it a Greek scale, a Chinese scale, or a Martian scale, can be put together in various combinations to create music with a sound characteristic of that culture.

Although Pythagoras' Chromatic scale (below) is the basis of Western civilization's

DO   di   **RE**   ri   **ME**   **FA**   fi   **SO**   si   **LA**   li   **TI**   **DO**

music, it is rarely used in its complete 12 note form. Instead, certain notes are chosen from it (usually six or seven) to form less complex new scales.

By the Middle Ages, two of these new scales had become far more popular than any of the others that had been tried. These two most popular scales were named the **major** and **minor** scales. Each has eight notes. But the way that each scale's octave distance is broken up is different. Thus the major and minor scales have a very different musical "feel" from each other.

The major scale eventually evolved as the basis for much of Northern and Western Europe's music. We might call it the "musical alphabet" for most German and English classical music, and some folk music. It tends to have a strong, brassy, bouncy feel to it. Even random playing of the major scale notes sounds good to us — because these notes are the most basic building blocks of our American musical heritage.

Do   **RE**   **ME**   **FA**   **SO**   **LA**   **TI**   **DO**

The minor scale evolved as the basis for much of Eastern Europe's music. It has a more plaintive or wistful quality, and we might consider it to be the alphabet of most Gypsy and Yiddish music, and some folk music as well.

DO   di   **RE**   ri   **FA**   **SO**   si   li   **DO**

There is one more musical alphabet we must learn about: The Afro - American Blues Scale. Its seven notes always sound "bluesy" when played together in any combination.

DO   ri   **FA**   fi   **So**   li   **DO**

Octave notes are different notes that sound almost the same. The "musical distance" between these octave notes is divided up in different ways. There are four ways of dividing up this musical distance that we need to be able to hear. They are called the major scale, the minor scale, the blues scale, and the chromatic scale. We can easily describe these scales by using syllables like DO, RE, and MI. Now listen to my scale demonstrations on the recording until they sound familiar.

We've Got Rhythm!

The Harvard Dictionary of Music states that "Rhythm may be broadly defined as everything pertaining to the duration quality (long-short) of musical sounds." Rhythm pervades our everyday life, from the beating of our heart, to the ticking of a clock, to the sound of our footfalls while we walk across the wooden floor. What do these three rhythms have in common? They are all examples of a **steady beat**, in which the time between each sound is exactly the same.

Rhythmic Articulation Exercises

Each of these exercises is based on a steady beat, so practice tapping your foot as you say "one two three four" along with me. Try to make sure that each tap occurs along with me, and try to catch a quick breath (br) in the spot indicated.

Please do each exercise in three ways.
- First, practice simply saying the articulation.
- Secondly, practice replacing each syllable of the articulation with a single puff of breath.
- Thirdly, if you can, either produce a whistle with each puff of air, or (for you most advanced types) actually articulate the whistle. If you can't articulate and whistle at the same time yet, don't worry (be happy). I'll cover this technique in the chapter on tone.

| Tah | Tah | Tah | Tah (br) | Tah | Tah | Tah | Tah (br) |
| Tuka | Tuka | Tuka | (br) | Tuka | Tuka | Tuka | (br) |

Swinging The Beat

Blues, jazz, and contemporary musicians often use a rhythmic technique known as swinging the beat. This involves breaking each tap of the foot used in a steady beat into two parts, the **downbeat** and the **upbeat**. The downbeat is the part of the beat in which the foot hits the floor. The upbeat is the part during which the foot rises up. Swinging of the beat is often used on triple tongued articulations, as I demonstrate. It involves saying the "tuh" part of each "tuketa" (the downbeat) both a bit louder and for a bit longer than the "keta" (upbeat) part. So instead of saying, for example:

"one and a two and a three and a four and a", we would say:

"**one**   and a **two**   and a **three**   and a **four!**".

Tu   keta   **Tu**   keta   **Tu**   keta   **Tuh (br)**

Advanced Rhythm Breath Practice

Practice catching a quick breath *during* a beat. Can you grab a fast inhale instead of saying "ka" in these eight beat rhythm patterns? Do it slowly at first, then speed up. Without losing the beat, of course. The second one is plenty hard!

Tuka Tuka Tuka Tuka Tuka Tuka Tuka Tu(br)

Tuketa Tuketa Tuketa Tuketa Tuketa Tuketa Tuketa Tuke(br)

Try these again after reading the breathing chapter, and especially the section on catching quiet breaths (page 35).

Advanced Rhythm Work With More Notes

After you've practiced using a series of tuketas on one tone, listen to my demonstration of swung tuketas using a melody similar to a popular jazz structure (somewhat like the song "Three Little Fishies". Notice how I use a different note for each tuketa. I also play around with the rhythm a bit. Try it!

A Good Reason To Whistle

Mr. Oscar Brand, musician, folklorist, and whistler, had an eminently practical reason for learning to whistle. As he puts it:

"I began whistling when I was very small, maybe three or four years old. I discovered that I could make a sharp sound that was annoying to older people. But I didn't do it continuously, not until I started using the outhouse at my father's farm. My father was a busy man, and he never fixed the lock on the outhouse door after it broke. As a consequence, I was always afraid that someone would come upon me in the outhouse. So whenever I heard any kind of sound, I'd start whistling — and I would whistle loud. That would make sure that anyone coming would know I was there!"

Part Two: Tools of the Trade

The following sections are written in tandem by me and Jason. I'll let Jason speak in his own voice most of the time (generous of me, eh?), and occasionally interrupt with comments and exercises of my own.

As I said in the preview, since each section presents a range of instruction, there are two ways that you can go through the material. You can read the beginning section of a chapter, do the beginning exercises, and then go on to the beginning section of the next chapter. Or you can read and do the beginning section, then continue on until the exercises become too difficult to do (for now), and simply read the rest before going on to the following chapter.

Every so often I will insert a summary box, to sum up the information in a section.

On Breathing

You can go for days without water, weeks without food, and months, years, or decades without sex or a job. But even a few short minutes without breathing is more than most of us will ever manage in this lifetime.

Breathing is, as Jason will amplify on below, even more important to the whistler than it is to the population at large. It may seem like a more commonplace and less fascinating subject than pitch, or special effects. But it is the basis upon which everything else you do is built (both whistle-wise, and in the rest of your life).

This chapter is pretty long, and if you're in a sweat to whistle you can skip over it if you absolutely must. But don't stay away for too long, because even the best whistler can benefit *enormously* from a conscious study of the respiratory process. And heeere's Jason!

When I wrote earlier that a little half hour coaching session transformed a man's whistling into Grand Champion material, I was telling the truth. I didn't need to teach him how to whistle. What he needed to do was to begin to direct his breath consciously to advance his art. Once he opened up his breathing capacity, the rest took care of itself.

It's as simple as this: breath is essential to good whistling. Shallow breathing makes for short phrases and small sound. Without proper breath support, tone is thin and lacks resonance. If shortness of breath leads you to push for the sound, the tone will be harsh and even shrill, and lack the free floating quality that makes for pleasing musical expression. Range will be limited, because the oomph you need to get into the higher range will not be there. You may be able to hail a cab, but you can be sure that it's not going to take you to Carnegie Hall.

How I Learned To Breathe

When I first began to whistle before audiences, my breath was rather shallow and not well under my control. I had never heard of another performing whistler, and a lot of people thought that I must be nuts or a fool (or both) to try such a thing . Fearful and insecure thoughts raced through my mind when performing, often overwhelming my concentration on the music itself. My knees shook so much that after only a few standing performances of breathy trembling sound I decided to spend the next 2 years whistling seated before the public so that I could begin to control the sound. I was so scared that I was holding my breath while simultaneously fighting to let it go. I gasped a lot, and my vibrato was often unmanageable. My performances may have been fascinating to experience, but they were not a musical pride and joy (especially for me).

It was only when I began to gain confidence in my art that my breath began to flow. I realized that if I were crazy, so be it. Besides, a lot of people were listening to me, so at least, if foolish or crazy, I was in good company. I decided to breathe deeply, look people straight in the eye and whistle my song.

How did I learn to breathe better? That's a good question. I was helped by quite a few diverse pursuits. I began doing yoga in 1970, and attended many yogic breathing classes. I studied dance for a few years (until I looked into the full-length mirror one too many times), and did special breath work with a dance therapist.

When I became involved in the human potential movement, I spent almost two years participating and training in Reichian therapy, a means of emotional release whose foundation lies in deep rapid non-stop breathing. I went through and later practiced Postural Integration, a form of deep connective tissue release similar to Rolfing, that specifically opened up my body and released a lot of tension in my chest, throat, neck and mouth.

I studied massage, and discovered how much more breath I had when I was relaxed. And finally, I began to swim almost daily. Blessed with a swimming technique that has inspired lifeguards to jump in and attempt a rescue, I have to work twice as hard as anyone else to get to the other side of the pool. Pretty it is not, but as swimming is the only exercise that combines muscular exertion with precise breath control, it contributes to a lot of lung power.

Diligence And Compassion

I tell you all this because I know that deep full breaths are the key to all good whistling. If you are serious about your whistling, you need to devote yourself diligently to the study of the breath, while being compassionate to yourself at the same time. This combination of diligence and compassion is necessary because learning to breathe deeply often involves unlearning literally a lifetime of old habits, and may take time — but it's worth it! The more deeply you allow yourself to breathe, the more you will be able to experience the richness and fullness of life, as well as the richness and fullness of your breathing tone.

In my case, even after doing all of the above body and mind work, I was still not yet satisfied with my breathing. When I began to work with my whistling teacher, I needed to put breath marks (places where one can stop and breathe without impairing the rhythmic flow of the piece) all over my music. I was frustrated, but that did not stop me. I simply whistled more and harder. Finally one day, just like that, the intercostal muscles beneath my ribcage heaved a sigh of relief and let go. When I went for my next lesson, I had to erase all the breath marks in my music because my lung capacity had deepened overnight! It may have taken years until my breath finally opened up, but when it did, my life as well as my whistling changed. There is no question but that the work was well worth it for me and my whistling, and I'd like to help you to do the same.

Breathing For Beginners:
Jason's Floor Exercise

It's easy to begin the process of opening up your breath. For most people, it is simply a case of paying attention. Most people are not so constricted and filled with fear as I was when I first began to whistle. Simply by watching your breath, and breathing with intention, your whistling will change. Once

you hear the difference that a full breath makes, you will want to breathe more deeply each time you whistle. Your motivation will increase, and you will cease to think of breathing as work. Your whistling will open up, and so will your life.

Here's how I suggest you begin. Dress in loose pants or a comfortable skirt, and be sure that nothing is pinching your waist. Lie on your back on the floor, and bend your knees so that you lower back and soles of your feet rest comfortably on the floor. If you are more comfortable with a pillow beneath your head, put one there. Put the dog outside, send the kids off to school, turn off the phone, and if necessary shut the door or pull down the shades. If you find that you relax more deeply with some soothing music playing softly in the background, put it on. Whatever is right for you, set up the situation so you can lie quietly and undisturbed on the floor.

After you allow yourself to lie still for a bit, you will notice your muscles relaxing as your body settles in. Great! Allow it to happen, and enjoy feeling peaceful and still. If thoughts should begin to draw your attention away from relaxation, just let them pass through and return to your sensations of lying at peace on the floor. It is not necessary to drive hundreds of miles to a vacation retreat or Zen Monastery to feel at one with yourself. You can do it right here, simply by lying quiet and still.

After your breath and your body are relaxed, slowly bring one hand to rest on your

How To
Whistle Like A Pro!

© & ℗ by David Harp, 1989
Soundsheet # 1: Side A

33 1/3 RPM MONAURAL

PLACE COIN HERE IF SOUNDSHEET SLIPS

CONTENTS OF THIS SIDE:
Introduction...Your First Whistle...
Everything You Ever Wished
You Knew About Music and Sound
But Were Afraid To Ask...
You've Got Rhythm!

MFD. IN U.S.A. BY

EVATONE® CLEARWATER, FL.
SOUNDSHEETS

105876-1A

How To
Whistle Like A Pro!

© & ℗ by David Harp, 1989
Soundsheet # 1: Side B

33 1/3 RPM
MONAURAL

PLACE COIN HERE IF
SOUNDSHEET SLIPS

CONTENTS OF THIS SIDE:
Using Your Music Theory...Whistling Major
Scales...Jumping Octaves...Minor and
Blues Scales...Chromatic Scales...
The Pros Strut Their Vibratos

MFD. IN U.S.A. BY EVATONE® CLEARWATER, FL.
105876-1B
SOUNDSHEETS

belly and the other to rest on your chest. Grow accustomed to them there, so that your feeling of relaxation deepens. Focusing only on your abdomen, begin to breathe deeply. Let your chest remain relaxed as you breathe into your abdomen. Concentrate solely on expanding your belly with air, then letting it go. Feel your hand rise and fall as you breathe. Observe how much air you can get into your belly, and how much it can expand. (No one is looking, so it's okay to open your top button and fill with so much air that you look positively pregnant). Breathe deeply, and observe your belly rising and falling as air moves through your body.

After you have done that for awhile, allow your breath to return to normal. Now focus on your chest, and repeat the process. Keeping your belly relaxed, fill your chest with air and then gently release it. Feel the air filling the entire upper part of your body. Send it into the sides of your rib cage, into your shoulders and the space between your shoulder blades. Feel your whole upper body filling with air, and then settling as the air is released.

As you do this, you may discover a part of your body that feels tight. If this occurs, consciously visualize your breath flowing into the tight area, and picture that area relaxing as you then exhale. With a bit of practice, you will begin to discover how controlling the breath can release tension in the body, and so make more room for the music to flow.

Now once again let yourself relax. When you are ready, begin to breathe first into your abdomen, and then continue your breathing until the breath moves up into your chest. You will find that your belly will flatten out some as the air goes up into the chest. As you continue the process, explore how much space you can fill with your breath.

There is no need to force. The breath will move as it will, and the body will open when the time is right. Whatever your capacity for breath may be, simply experience it first filling your belly, and then filling your chest.

After practicing breathing lying down for awhile, let the breath return to normal.

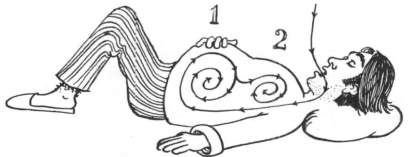

Making sure that you are not dizzy, roll onto your side and use your hands to come to a sitting position. This helps you maintain a relaxed state. Slowly come to a standing position. Now repeat the entire sequence, using your hands on your chest and belly to help guide and encourage the breath.

Practice this sequence daily if possible until it becomes easy for you. It takes time to retrain yourself, and to break old habits. Be easy on yourself, and stick with it.

Too Much Of A Good Thing: On Hyperventilation

A few people sometimes find that they get light headed or dizzy when they begin exploring deepening their breath. If they continue breathing deeply, their fingers may begin to tingle and their lips and fingers begin to contract. This is called hyperventilation. Do not be scared if it happens to you; there is nothing wrong with you (but please do read the "Two Notes", below). Hyperventilation is a sign that you are not accustomed to processing so much oxygen, and it will pass.

Sometimes when I work with people who hyperventilate so easily that we cannot really get very far, I allow them to enter into the state and then bring them back by putting a paper bag over their nose and mouth and instructing them to breathe their own carbon dioxide. The reason for pushing your limits by entering into this uncomfortable state (at least occasionally) is simple.

As in all forms of exercise, it is the act of pushing the muscles beyond their normal capabilities that develop them. Your payoff will be in the form of increased breathing capacity, better whistling, and healthier living.

Two Notes:

As we said in the front of the book, if you have any physical problems, are pregnant, or are under the care of a physician for any reason: please ask her or him about this program *before* beginning it. This is especially important regarding any exercises that cause you to hyperventilate. Since any form of breathing exercise is health-giving for most people, your caregiver will probably encourage you to go ahead, and may even join you!

Also, never whistle to the point of hyperventilation while standing up, driving, operating heavy equipment, or sitting on the edge of the Grand Canyon. For pleasure, you can just as easily whistle without using much volume, and avoid any risk of passing out in an embarrassing position!

When I work with people one-on-one, I sometimes discover that people who breathe just great on the floor start gasping for breath and breathing every few notes once they stand up and start to whistle. At that point, I may suggest that they stop whis-

tling, and return to just breathing. Only when the foundation becomes solid do we move on to music making.

Of course, you are going to be eager to whistle. I don't expect you to spend the next month just practicing breathing without wanting to immediately begin applying what you have learned to whistling. But there are ways that you can continue your breath practice as you begin to funnel the breath into sound, as we'll discuss in the Intermediate Breath section.

Some In-Action Advice From David

• While you whistle, try to remember to breathe from your stomach. It sometimes helps me to keep one hand on my belly, while pretending that it is a magnet that pulls my stomach outward. Unflattering though it may be, I let it be okay for my belly to pouch out as much as it wants to, and to fill up before any air enters my chest. When exhaling, I gently push in with my hand to remind me to release all the air from my stomach.

• A warning: although it is important to take in plenty of air during a breath, don't overdo it. If you are too full, the first few notes whistled on that breath will come out too fast, and be hard to control.

• Good posture encourages good breathing. Sit or stand up straight. Your shoulders should be neither drooping nor raised (which they will tend to do during the difficult passages, or when you are running out of breath). Keep your chin pointing straight ahead (not up or down), this helps the airway stay most open. Here's a before-whistling exercise that will help.

• Tighten and then completely relax your jaws a few times. Then do the same with your shoulders, arms, and hands. Rotate your head from left to right as far as is comfortable. Gently swing your arms at your sides while relaxing your shoulders, and visualize yourself shaking any remaining tension off the ends of your fingers, like tiny beads of sweat. You can do this so casually that no one will even notice — and then be ready to whistle like a pro!

Intermediate Breath: Quiet Control

One essential part of good whistling is to learn how to take deep breaths quickly without making a lot of noise. There is no point in whistling "Singin' in the Rain" if the breaths you take between phrases sound like you're actually running from a fast approaching tornado. Listen to yourself, and record yourself—you'll quickly learn to hear the difference between a quiet and a noisy breath.

On Working With David

Let me tell you about how David and I worked together. When David came to me for his first lesson, we made an interesting discovery. Although he is a master blues harmonica player with a world-wide reputation, I was amazed to discover that David had never really developed a capacity for long sustained breaths. Harmonica players, it seems, move breath in and out through the instrument without removing their mouth from it. Harmonica players may not need to take long deep breaths to make great music, because they can make music while breathing both in and out. While it builds the foundation for great breathing technique, harmonica playing does not necessarily call for deep sustained breaths.

Because of his commitments to writing and publishing 25 books and attending 30 conferences and 5 blues festivals in 65 days, plus changing his new baby's diapers and doing psychological and meditation counseling whenever possible, David could take only a few lessons with me before going off to practice on his own. (Editor's note: Jason is being sarcastic here. I only had to write and publish three books, go to two conferences, and one blues festival in the two months we had to work together. I did change plenty of diapers... dh) So my mission was to reprogram his breathing pattern, plus to share 1000 other pointers in a very limited amount of time. I therefore packed a lot into a few lessons.

After we moved from breath practice on the floor to whistling while standing, I had David put one hand on his belly and the other on his chest. I would instruct him to take a quiet deep breath, whistle a complete phrase, stop, consciously and quietly bring the breath back into the belly and chest, and then whistle the next phrase. Whenever he would forget to breathe deeply, and just take a short little breath (which, harmonica-player-like, he did all the time), I would interrupt him and return his attention to his breathing. If between phrases he would gasp or make a lot of noise, we would pause and he would relax his jaw and throat before breathing in. Occasionally I would stand behind him and massage the back of his neck or move his head around (although this was difficult because he's taller than me). Sometimes I would allow him to struggle with a phrase on just a short amount of breath, and then have him repeat it after taking a full breath. He would immediately hear the difference!

David's Hints On Quiet Breathing

As Jason described, I have trouble with quick and quiet inhalations. We harmonica players are used to grabbing our inhales through the harp, and a wailing chord can hide even the loudest gasp or throat noise. So when I began to study whistling, I had to learn a whole new set of skills.

Taking a quiet breath involves learning to relax the entire throat, including the soft palate. As you may remember from the mouth exploration, tightening and raising the soft palate at the back of the throat closes off the nasal cavity. Relaxing it does the opposite.

The feeling that you have when your throat is open and relaxed is best likened to the sensation of yawning. The entire throat feels open, and you can feel the coolness of the entering breath all down your gullet.

When taking a quiet breath:

• Allow the soft palate to open, so that air can come in from both nose and mouth.

• Keep your teeth at least half or three-quarters of an inch apart, or you'll hear the sound of the air rushing past your front teeth.

• Keep your lips wide apart, and don't allow them to be pulled in towards your teeth by the incoming breath.

• Think yawn.

As Jason helped me to do, stop yourself between phrases if you have to, and deliberately practice taking full quiet breaths.

By breaking music down into phrases, and practicing what he needed to do to bring each one together into a beautiful sounding piece, David began to learn what good whistling is all about. Because he had such a strong musical sense and solid background, David was able to take all I had taught him back home to frequent practice. As he explored teaching whistling to others, he observed the places where they needed work, and learned in turn. Hence a whistler was born.

You can do the same for yourself. It's simply a matter of working with the breath. And you have a head start. It's the first thing you did when you emerged from the womb, and it's the last thing you'll do before moving on. You're already an expert. You just have to remember what breathing is all about.

Advanced Breathing Exercises:

The following are some advanced techniques and exercises. But please feel free to try them, even if you're a beginner. They may tend to induce hyperventilation, so please re-read my warning on page 34, and do them sitting down!

The Big Breath Exercises

An average amount of air exchanged during a normal breath can be as low as one half a quart. Yet as many as three, four, or even five quarts of air can be exchanged with practice.

An exercise that I occasionally do is to take a deep breath, then count as high as I can get on the exhale. Pronounce each syllable of each number clearly, in a normal speaking voice. On a good breath, I can break 100 now. It's taken a bit of practice!

As a variation, use multiple puffs of air in place of spoken numbers. And, once in a while, time yourself and see how long you can maintain a whistle tone for. This will depend, of course, on how loud you're whistling. I haven't gotten much beyond half a minute, yet, and have been embarrassed to ask the pros how long they can go for (or perhaps embarrassed to hear their answer!).

For another variation, which helps control of breath as well as volume, place a candle a few inches in front of your face. Pucker and blow gently on it, so that it keeps flickering but doesn't go out. Try it with the candle at different distances. This is a traditional flute player's exercise, but good for us whistlers, too.

In-Whistling

It is possible, if not too commonly practiced, to whistle on the inhale. Joel Brandon, 1987 Grand Champion of the International Whistle-Off, does all of his whistling on the inhale. He reportedly uses a traditional African method of producing an in-whistle. Although we talked briefly by phone, he was, unfortunately, the only Grand Champion of the last five years from whom I was unable to obtain either information or a recording before this book had to go to press. I hope to see him at the Whistle-Off this year, and to have more information on his style in a subsequent edition of this method.

I usually use inhale whistling just to catch a quick breath in the middle of a long or complicated passage. The tone of my in-whistle is worse than on my out-whistle, and I find that if I do not push out my lower jaw slightly when I change from out to in, my whistle goes up slightly in pitch. The tongue position seems to stay the same.

Practice changing from an out-whistle to an in-whistle without changing either pitch or tone. It's a real challenge, but it may help you get through a tough piece of music some day!

The Breath Meditation

Begin by practicing this meditation while sitting comfortably in a quiet place, back straight, feet flat on floor, hands in lap.

Simply count the exhale of each breath, mentally: "Inhale...1, Inhale...2, Inhale...3, Inhale...4", then begin again with "Inhale...1." Do it once now, before reading any further.

Continue reading these instructions, and try this simple meditation some more. Strive not to lose the count, and also try not to alter or regularize your breathing in any way. See if you can feel the physical sensation of each breath, both inhale and exhale, as it passes through your nose or mouth. Does this breath feel warm, or cool? Is it a quick breath, or a slow one?

If you find yourself thinking about anything except the feel of your breath and the number of that breath, return to focus on the sensation of breathing, and on the number of the breath. If you are not absolutely sure what number breath you're on, immediately begin again with "Inhale...1." No judging, no "I blew the count" thoughts, just back to "Inhale...1."

When enjoying a favorite hobby, like making model ships or sewing, or even whistling, your thoughts generally focus directly on just what you're doing. Glueing wood, or stitching, become your "preferred" thoughts. Right now, consider the counting of each breath and how each breath feels to be your "preferred" thoughts. So other thoughts such as memories, plans, fears, desires, lunch, or whatever else will just be gently replaced by your "Inhale...1, Inhale...2" and so on, as soon as you notice them creeping in. And they will! Of course it's difficult to stay focussed! But strangely satisfying, as it becomes more natural.

The beauty of this meditation is that, once learned, you can do it anywhere! Try it on the bus, or during a long, boring meeting. Like all meditations designed to clear the mind, with a bit of practice the breathing meditation gives rise to a delightfully peaceful and calm feeling. Using a meditation of this type to clear the mind can also be most useful to your whistling — but I'll talk more about that in the chapter entitled "Zen And The Art Of Whistling", on page 73.

Breath And Music

It's impossible to whistle many pieces without stopping for breath. But if we've prepared in advance, we can plan our breaths to do as little violence to the music as possible. Working with the rhythm exercises (page 28) will help you to know how to "steal" breaths without changing the rhythm during a long note, or between two notes that are the same. And now I'll let Jason have the final word on high performance breathing.

Paying attention to the flow of the musical line and to the sound of the breath is essential to good whistling. I take my breaths in a way that breathes life into a musical phrase rather than cutting it in two.

If at times I cannot whistle a whole phrase without taking a breath, I work with my accompanist to leave enough space for me to take a quick catch-up breath without breaking the flow of the music. And in those cases when I perform to recorded orchestral accompaniment that simply does not allow enough space for sufficient breath, I draw in as much air as I possibly can, silently ask my audience for forgiveness, and follow my gasp with a flood of sound that hopefully washes all my noisy breaths away.

Most whistlers have some breath noise in concert, and even in the studio it is difficult to rid the recording of all the respiration. So rather than worrying about exorcising such sounds, we merely try to minimize them, using the techniques that David and I have described.

The Conti-1 and its Inventor

On Pitch

Yes, that last chapter was a long one. But it needed to be wordy, since there just isn't much information about breathing that can be conveyed in a recording. It's tempting to say that if you've heard one breath, you've heard 'em all — but of course we whistlers try to avoid having *anyone* hear our breaths!

As you doubtless recall from my preview, pitch refers to the high-low quality of a sound. Please listen repeatedly to the recording, and read as much of this chapter as you choose. If you feel like you need to do a lot of work on pitch, you should probably read it all. Now it's time to start applying some of the music theory information that we've learned!

Pitch For Beginners

Since much of the work that we must do with pitch takes place in the ears and the mind rather than the mouth, this section actually begins in the music theory section on page 22. Reread it, and listen to the music theory sections on SoundSheet # 1-A. And, of course, if you haven't gotten your whistle yet, you can use your voice on the exercises, or just listen and learn.

You will need to learn to hear pitches in your "mind's ear" before you can translate them into the actual whistle pitches produced by the mouth. So after you've listened to the music theory section, begin

listening to the scales presented at the beginning of SoundSheet # 1-B.

Matching Tones

This is just basically a matter of practice. Review the pictures of lower note tongue position and higher note tongue position, and then listen to the practice tones, and to yourself trying to match them.

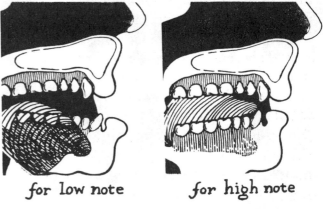

for low note   *for high note*

At first, *of course* your tone will be a bit higher or lower than the tone that you are trying to match. But by listening closely, and studying (without whistling) the music theory recording, your ears will become more sensitive, so that you will eventually be able to tell whether your whistled note is higher or lower than the piano note. Then it becomes a matter of adjusting your tongue position to match the highness or lowness of the piano note.

When your note is higher or lower, it will be quite clear that there are two notes occurring (yours and the piano recording). When the two notes match, they will just seem to sound "right" together. There will only seem to be one note, since even though the sound quality of a whistle and of a keyboard differ, the matching pitch tends to overwhelm any other sound differences. So learn to make fine back and forth, up and down adjustments of your tongue, until only one note seems to ring forth!

Some of you may suspect that you are whistling a note one octave lower or higher than mine. If so, it will sound "right" also. Please don't worry about using the wrong octave note right now, as we'll be working on octave jumping a lot more, soon.

For Real Beginners

If you've only recently been able to get any whistle sound at all, now is the time to experiment with raising and lowering your tone. Use the lower and higher tongue positions to see how much you can change your tone, and don't worry if you can only get two or three notes at first. Read the Pitch section, at least up to the intermediate part, and listen to the recording a few times. Then do the following.

Start on your lowest tone, and see if you can pick out and whistle the first few notes of "Frere Jacques". Then start on your highest tone, and whistle the first notes of "Three Blind Mice". Practice. Lots. Soon you'll be able to produce three recognizable tones.

The first complete song that you'll be able to play is a simplified version of "Mary Had A Little Lamb". It requires only three notes, DO, RE, and MI. Begin on your highest note (your MI) for the first syllable "Mar". Begin the song. When you come to the third time that the words "little lamb" are repeated, don't worry about raising your tone for the syllables "tle lamb". Just stay on your highest note, which you will have hit for the syllable "lit", and articulate the words "tle lamb" on that *same* note. Then finish the song. And don't worry. As your range expands, you'll be able to play more exciting songs!

Your Whistling Range

The four octave range in the picture following will probably cover all of the notes that anyone reading this book can whistle. Many amateur whistlers have a usable range of only a bit over one octave. Most pros have at least two. A three octave usable range is very rare. Ripley's Believe-It-Or-Not (I don't) reportedly lists a whistler with a three-and-a-half octave range. We'll figure out your best range, then expand it, later on.

In just a month or so of practice I've expanded my range from a weak-toned one-and-a-quarter octave to nearly three! Of course, my bottom two notes and my top five or six are totally unreliable, but I can hit them (on a good day, after warming up) at times, and eventually will be able to use at least some of them on demand if I'm lucky. And even without the questionable lows and highs, I now have a usable two octaves. With a bit of diligence, and the willingness to sound bad when practicing, you can expand your range similarly!

Low, Medium, And High Major Scales

The brackets in the picture below indicate the beginning and ending notes of the low, medium, and high major scales. Try matching tones with these. Which one feels most comfortable to you? Why don't you try them all?

Listen to me match the tones of the medium scale. Can you hear that my whistle tone for the seventh note of the scale (TI) was a bit lower than the piano tone? I adjusted it upwards almost instantly, but listening to my mistake will help you to hear the subtleties of matching tones (I wish I could claim that I did it on purpose for just that reason, but that would be fibbing).

Pitch Intervals

Some people find it easier to hear pitches in the context of a song, rather than as scales. So I have provided songs whose beginning notes represent the distances, or intervals, between different notes of the scale. If this doesn't seem useful to you, just keep listening to my recordings, and forget about this for a while. This section is not on the tape, as I hope that you know most of these songs already.

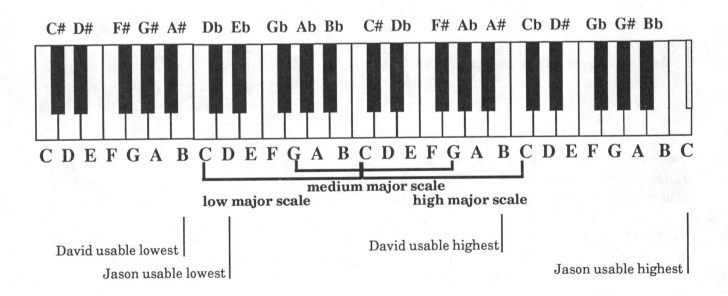

This first two notes of this song represent the jump from a low octave note to the next higher one, as discussed in the following section:

DO   (RE MI FA SO LA TI)   DO
Some ——————————————————— where (over the rainbow)

These next three songs can all be used to learn either the first two or three notes of the major scale:

DO RE MI DO   DO RE MI   DO RE MI MI
Fre re Jac ques   Dan ny Boy   Al lou et te

Following are songs whose first notes represent a variety of commonly used pitch intervals:

DO MI FA SO   DO FA   DO DO SO SO
Oh When The Saints   For auld (acquaintance)   Twinkle Twinkle

DO fi SO   DO ri FA SO LA   DO LA SO
Ma ri a   A las my lo ve   My bon nie

And this last song can be most helpful for learning the descending major scale:
DO TI LA SO   FA MI RE DO
Joy to the world the lord has come

Just as an aside: Want to impress other musicians? Instead of using the syllable or solmi terms, use number names for notes. Oh no! Another way of referring to notes? Yes, but this one is pretty easy. It's based on the seven notes of the major scale. Each note gets a number. So DO is 1, RE is 2, ME is 3, FA is 4, SO is 5, LA is 6, and TI is 7. Flat and sharp notes are indicated by the usual # and b symbols (for example, the note di between DO [1] and RE [2] could be either #1 or b2), so the entire chromatic scale would look like this:

DO di RE ri ME FA fi So si LA li TI DO
1   #1/b2   2   #2/b3   3   4   #4/b5   5   #5/b6   6   #6/b7   7   8

Mental Training

Scientists like my friend Dr. Charlie Garfield, originator of the Peak Performance techniques, have proven that visualizing as clearly as possible what you wish to later perform can help you to do so. So spend some time visualizing, or creating a clear mental picture, of yourself whistling.

There are many different levels on which this can be done. If you are a pre-whistler, visualize yourself patiently working with tongue and lip position until you obtain that first tone. If you are an intermediate whistler, spend some time listening to the scales and octave jumps while visualizing yourself whistling them. If you're an advanced whistler, carefully visualize that next lowest or next highest note becoming clearer and clearer.

No matter what your level, you may want to spend some time just listening to the pro whistlers' selections, while visualizing the sounds issuing from your own lips.

All of these exercises will be more effective if you are in a relaxed state, so I suggest doing a few moments of breathing meditation (page 38) before doing the visualization exercise.

Intermediate Pitch
Octave Jumping

Octave notes are basically notes that have a very similar sound quality. This is because one of the notes is caused by vibrations exactly twice as fast as the vibrations of the other note. If that last sentence seemed confusing, please feel free to reread the music theory section, and you'll remember plenty about the hows and whys of octaves. The "some——where" example from the song "Somewhere Over The Rainbow", described in the Pitch Interval section above, will also help.

Many whistlers have a fairly limited range of pitch compared to most other instruments (pianos have more than seven octaves, harmonicas and guitars at least three). Many decent amateur whistlers have far less than two octaves, sometimes only one-and-a-third or one-and-a-half. Since some songs require a two octave range, learning to jump up or down from one octave note to another allows us to play songs that would otherwise be out of our range.

Whether you're a low ranger, medium ranger, or high ranger, try all of the indicated octave jumps, from the bottom C to the top C of the low major scale, from the bottom G to the top G of the medium major scale, and from the bottom C to the top C of the high major scale. If you're a high ranger, experiment with doing your high C to C octave jump along with the low ranger C to C jump on the recording. Low rangers, try matching your low C to C octave jump with the high ranger C to C jump on the recording. As I said before, even though you are one octave lower or higher than the recording, it should sound pretty "right". Middle rangers, see if you can match tones with either or both of the other jumps.

Remember, these octave jumps require large tongue movements. The bulk of your tongue may actually move as much as 3/4 of an inch or more as you jump octaves.

And if you're embarrassed about sounding bad — well, just listen to my feeble attempts to match the higher C of the high range jump!

The Major Scale Octave Jump

Now it's time to use octave jumps not by themselves, but while whistling a major scale. Listen to my low, medium, and high examples, then try a few. Here are the notes that we'll be using.

DO RE MI FA SO LA TI DO

If you're a low ranger, make sure to also try the medium and even the high major scale octave jumps. It will be easier for you to do the medium major scale *with* the jump than it was to do the high major scale without the jump. Even though the medium major with jump and high major without jump share the first five notes, the jump knocks off the three highest notes, – a real blessing for me, as you can easily hear!

Mediums, try the low and high jump majors, because the jump may just put them within your range.

Highs, see if you can match the notes of the medium major octave jump. The lower notes after the jump may be a challenge!

You should probably try to whistle some major scales with octave jumps in as many places as possible. Some possibilities (not recorded) might be:

		DO	RE	MI	FA	SO	LA
TI	DO			or			

				DO	RE	MI	FA
SO	LA	TI	DO		or		

DO	RE	MI	FA	SO	LA	TI
DO			or			

					DO	RE
MI	FA	SO	LA	TI	DO	

There's one more. Why don't you try to identify it and whistle it by yourself?

Using Octave Jumps In Songs

Experiment! Take a song like "On Top Of Old Smoky", and begin it on a note that seems fairly high to you. Then, instead of going up between the words "Old" and "Smo", jump down to the lower octave "Smo", and then down again to the "key". We might represent this in graph form. The words on the left are the usual way of playing the song. The words on the right show how it would look when whistled as I just described it.

```
DO: (higher)        Smo
TI:                 / \
LA:                /   key
SO:         Old         Old
FA:         /          /
MI:       of         of
RE:       /          /
DO: On top      On top      Smo
TI:                            \
LA: (lower)                     key
```

Here are a few other suggestions for songs in which to use octave jumps. Start "Swing Low Sweet Chariot" on a note near the middle of your range. Instead of trying to go down between the notes "chari" and "o-ot" (which might easily be out of your range, since the song goes down nearly an octave in the first four words), jump *up* an octave to find the "o" and "ot" notes.

"Happy Birthday" normally requires a minimum range of an octave and a half. But if you start on a high end note, and then jump down nearly an octave to whistle the third syllable "birth", you can do the song with a range of just one octave. Try it. It's not exactly traditional, but it works!

Using The Major Scale

Practicing the major scale will help you to play a *tremendous* amount of music, as it is the single most popular scale used by our culture. Much folk music (except for the folk music of the Gypsy, Jewish, and Eastern European cultures) is based on the major scale, as is a great deal of classical and contemporary music. And most of what is not based on the major scale will be covered by our next two scales.

Advanced Work On Pitch

The minor and blues scales are no harder to whistle than the major. However, for some whistlers, they may be less familiar. If this is the case for you, spend lots of time listening to the recorded portions on music theory and pitch, and pay special attention to the recorded minor selections "Blue Mockingbird" and "Greensleeves", and to "House Of The Rising Sun", which uses a combination of blues scale and minor scale notes. Its first verse is bluesier, and the second verse has a more minor flavor.

The Mournful Minor Scale

The plaintive tones of the minor scale lend piquancy to classics as diverse as "Summertime", "Autumn Leaves", "When Johnny Comes Marching Home", and "The Volga Boatmen".

Here's what the solmi notes look like (under a full chromatic scale), to refresh your memory. Try the low, medium, and high octaves. Each begins and ends on the same note as did your low, medium, and high major scales, although some of the middle notes are different from those of the major.

DO	di	RE	ri	ME	FA	fi	SO	si	LA	li	TI	DO
DO		RE	ri		FA		SO	si		li		DO

Minor Scale Octave Jumps

The idea is the same as it was for the major scale. After you've practiced and learned a regular minor scale, try it with an octave jump somewhere in its middle. Listen to my recorded example, and experiment. Use octave jumps to vary the minor songs listed above.

DO RE ri FA

SO si li DO

The Blues Scale

Ahhh...my favorite. As a professional blues harmonicist, this scale has been my muse, my love, and my bread and butter for the last twenty years. It's so beautiful that I can't stand to play it as just a cold, dry, scale. So in my scale demonstrations I've added just a bit of rhythm to the notes of the scale. And here's an equation as momentous, to me, and more positive in application, as Einstein's $E = mc^2$: **notes plus rhythm equal music**.

DO		ri		FA	fi	SO		li		DO

Listen to my low, medium, and high blues scales and learn to play them. On each one, I go up the scale in a steady beat, then come down in a bluesy little rhythm. Apply rhythms of your own as you whistle the scale, and you'll be creating your own improvisations.

The Blues Scale Octave Jump

It's basically the same as the major or minor octave jump, applied to the blues scale. Try some blues scales with octave jumps in different places. My example looks like this.

DO ri FA fi SO

li DO

Blues/Jazz Improvisation

The blues scale is at the heart and soul of blues/jazz improvisation. If you practice it, with application of rhythm, you can just make up long sequences of scale notes that have a pleasing, melodic feel, even if they have no real tune.

But jamming, or improvising, with other musicians is perhaps the most satisfying way to go. After you have mastered the blues scale, try whistling blues scales along with your local blues radio station. Try to make the first note of your blues scale match the first note of the song, if possible. After a while, this will become natural.

Or try jamming along with Ugo Conti on his version of "House Of The Rising Sun" on SoundSheet # 2-B. He is playing in the key of A, which means that you'll need to whistle a blues scale just a bit higher than our medium blues scale (which is in the key of G). Try to match the first note of your scale with his first guitar chord. As a hint, Jason's last long note is a Bb, just a touch higher than the note you want for jamming with Ugo. Of course, if you are going to match Jason's tone, feel free to be one or even two octaves beneath him!

Songs And Range

If songs always began on the lowest note that would be used in that song, it would be easy to know what note to begin a song on. We would just start on our deepest tone, and then whistle away, content in the knowledge that we'd be able to hit every note, since few songs have more than a one-and-a-half or at most two octave range. However, although many songs do begin on their lowest note, not all do.

For that reason, it's often important to start a song on a note that is low enough so that you can go as high as you need to in order to reach all the notes, but high enough so that you can go as low as you need to hit the low notes. Now that you can use octave jumps, you have an alternative way of dealing with low and high notes. But it's best not to use octave jumps if you can avoid them (judges at the whistling contests tend to look down on excessive octave jumping, and a song usually will sound best when played as originally written).

So when considering a new song:

• I usually begin to whistle it starting on a note one or two notes above my lowest usable tone.

• To locate that note, I whistle my lowest tone and think DO.

• Then I whistle RE MI, hold the MI note, and begin the song on my low MI.

• If I eventually hit a note that is too high for me, I then know that I'm probably out of luck, since I started pretty near my bottom note.

• If the too-high note seems almost but not quite within my usable grasp, I may do the first three bulleted steps again, but start the song on RE instead of MI. I gain one note that way on the high end.

• If I eventually hit a note that is too low for me, I repeat the first three steps, but start the song on my low FA or even SO note.

Expanding Your Range: High

There are two aspects to expanding your range — the highs and the lows. You will want to expand in both directions. This

How To
Whistle Like A Pro!

© & ℗ by David Harp, 1989
Soundsheet # 2: Side A

33 1/3 RPM MONAURAL

PLACE COIN HERE IF SOUNDSHEET SLIPS

CONTENTS OF THIS SIDE:
The Amazing Warble...The Pros Strut Their
Warbles...Ornaments...Calling All Birds...
Milton Briggs: *Whistler's Polka &
Blue Mockingbird*...Marge Carlson:
On Wings Of Song...David's
Frere Jacques

MFD. IN U.S.A. BY

105876-2A

EVATONE® CLEARWATER, FL.
SOUNDSHEETS

How To
Whistle Like A Pro!

© & ℗ by David Harp, 1989
Soundsheet # 2: Side B

33 1/3 RPM
MONAURAL

PLACE COIN HERE IF
SOUNDSHEET SLIPS

CONTENTS OF THIS SIDE:

Jason Serinus: *Jeannie With The Light Brown Hair & Ernanie* (Verdi)...Dr. Ugo Conti: *House Of The Rising Sun & Synthesizer Dandy*...Roy Thoreson: *Greensleeves*...Dr. Jack Cohen: *Strike The Viol* (Purcell)...Bob Larson: *Battle Hymn Of The Republic*...David's Goodbye

MFD. IN U.S.A. BY EVA-TONE® SOUNDSHEETS CLEARWATER, FL.
105876-2B

is my favorite exercise for expanding my high range.

- Begin on your lowest usable note.
- Go up the major scale, note by note, until you can't go any higher. With any luck, you will need to go into the next octave.
- When you reach your highest note that sounds reasonably clear, try to hit the next note, even though it squeaks, cracks, or just hisses — which it will. This is just the first step. With practice, you'll make that mutinous note usable.
- Hitting this next note will involve tightening your lips, holding your cheeks in tightly, and perhaps bracing the tip of your tongue against your lower front teeth. This will leave only a tiny open space (perhaps the size of a pea) between the top front part of your tongue and your upper front teeth (and between your tongue and the space between your upper and lower teeth, through which the air escapes).
- Experiment with air volume (probably higher than normal) and position, and try to locate the combination that will produce that next highest note.
- Warming up will help. Play lots of scales or songs before doing range work.

Expanding Your Range: Low

I believe that a key to expanding range in the lower direction is to practice the descending major scale. As I said in the Pitch Interval section, the song "Joy To The World" begins with a complete, one octave descending major scale.

- Begin on your highest usable note.
- Go down the major scale note by note, until you can't go any lower. With any luck, you will need to go down into the next octave.
- When you reach your lowest note that sounds reasonably clear, try to hit the next note, even though it comes out mostly as air, no sound. Again, this is just the first step.
- Hitting this next note will involve dropping your jaw, and pulling your tongue so far back that you may almost gag.
- Your lip hole must stay round, but relaxed. You will probably have to consciously raise your lower lip to keep a round hole after your jaw is dropped.
- Lower your air volume dramatically. You will obtain the note almost inaudibly at first. You will hear the sound of the air exiting your lips at least as loudly as the whistle tone when you begin to work with it.

When you first add a note to your range, it will be flaky, weak, and unreliable. Squeaky and hissy if high, nearly soundless if low. Like *my* high C and low Ab are now. In a word: awful. Don't let that stop you. Eventually you will make the note usable, if you continue to work with it.

The Chromatic Scale (for serious students only!)

Spend some time listening to the chromatic scale, without even trying to whistle along at first. Since the notes of the chromatic scale are equally spaced, you can begin and end anywhere in this two octave sequence. After you've done enough listening (why not use the visualization and relaxation techniques discussed earlier?), begin trying to whistle a chromatic scale. When you start to be able to whistle segments of a chromatic scale, see if you can match your notes with the ones in the recording. Eventually you may be able to match the entire two chromatic scales. It will take plenty of practice. It's worth it. But don't worry about this exercise until you have done everything else in the Pitch chapter.

For Fanatics Only

Here are three really hard things to do, if you've mastered everything else.

Go back to the Pitch Intervals and practice each one separately, by whistling. Then do this drill:

DO RE DO MI DO FA DO SO DO LA DO TI DO

Practice the first two notes (easy), then the first four (not quite so easy), then the first six, and so on. When you can do the entire sequence, perform it from right to left as well. When both ways become easy, go for this one:

DO di DO RE DO ri DO MI DO FA DO fi DO SO DO si DO LA DO li DO TI DO

Do it left to right and right to left too.

Play one of the major, minor, or blues scales, and whistle along with it. Put your hand on the volume control of the tape deck (or the record player, but I do hope you've put the recordings on cassette by now). Practice playing the first note of the scale, then turning the sound off for a few seconds while you continue to whistle the rest of the scale. Turn the sound back on, and see if you are still in tune and on time. This is a wonderful exercise for both rhythm and pitch.

Feeling confident or masochistic? Buy a guitar tuner. Make sure it is one that will work when whistled into. It will have a dial or set of lights that will tell you when you are *perfectly* on pitch. It will be frustrating at first, because it is hard to hold a whistle on pitch as precisely as a guitar. If you work with it, it will force you to stay on pitch. They're expensive, so try one out in the music store before you buy it...

Tone And Tonal Techniques

Since it is far easier to learn about tone by listening than by reading about it, this chapter needs fewer words. The most important part of this information can be found on the Sound-Sheets. Please listen lots, both to my instruction and to the recording of the pros.

Beginning Tone Control

Practice hitting a single note and staying on it. Don't be afraid to spend plenty of time doing just that. And listen to yourself, or tape record yourself. If you find yourself getting a breathy sound, you probably have one of two problems.

• Your teeth may be too close together (they should be no less than one-third of an inch apart).

• Or your throat may not be relaxed. Think about how your throat feels when you yawn. It feels very open on the inside.

• You generally want to prevent your cheeks from billowing out as you whistle, as this may change the pitch of a note unexpectedly. So keep just enough tension in them so that they don't puff out with air.

Staccato And Legato Attacks

You can move from one note to the next in either of two ways.

Sliding from one to the other is called a legato attack. Making each note sound clearly and separately provides a staccato attack.

• In a legato attack, your air is expelled in a steady stream, and only your tongue moves when the pitch changes.

• For an easy staccato attack, you can begin each note sharply with a quick puff of air from your lungs.

• For an even sharper staccato attack, use your epiglottis (the flap of skin covering your windpipe) to emit a tiny and controlled cough-like blast of air to begin each note. Practice coughing to identify the sensation of opening and closing the windpipe with the epiglottis.

• Beware of "coughing" too vigorously and letting out a "kuh" sound with each whistle note.

Attack Exercises

• Spend some time on just one note, experimenting with staccato attacks.

• Go back to the rhythm exercises and practice them with a staccato attack.

• Practice some simple songs or scales using legato and staccato attacks.

• Eventually learn to do rapid legato and staccato scales without sacrificing accuracy of pitch. Start slow, then build up to high speed.

• Jigs, fiddle tunes, and many classical pieces of music can provide great opportunities for staccato practice. Dr. Cohen's classical selection demonstrates great use of stacatto notes.

• Keep your throat relaxed, and listen carefully to your tonal quality. Read the section entitled "A Few Last Words On Tone" at the end of this chapter.

Dynamics

This word refers the use of loudness and softness in a piece of music. It's boring to have all of our notes at the same volume level. Practice dynamic control by:

• Taking a single note and making it louder and softer, while maintaining good tone and a steady pitch.

• Play a song or a scale, consciously raising and lowering the volume at the times that seem most appropriate to you. Does the song or scale need to build up to a grand finale? Or to fade gently away? Try it both ways.

• Study the way in which the pros use dynamic control in their songs. Who uses lots of dynamic changes? Who doesn't? What kind of music seems to call for a lot of dynamic change? What kind calls for less?

Intermediate Tone

The following special tone effects are some of the most difficult things that whistlers do. Therefore my demonstrations are meant only to give you an idea of what you might sound like when you first begin to practice them (like I'm doing now). I'll allow

the experts to provide the serious (or, in Jason's case, the Serinus) examples.

The Vibrato

The standard vibrato is a tone effect involving what the trusty Harvard Dictionary Of Music calls "a minute fluctuation of pitch" (they clearly have not heard my vibrato yet). This can be accomplished with the tongue, by making a tiny, rapid, and very consistently controlled motion, like whispering "you you you".

The farther that the tongue moves when "you"ing, the more the pitch will change. Better whistlers tend to prefer a smaller pitch change (too little, of course, cannot be perceived), and keep the tongue from moving too far by bracing the tonguetip against the lower front teeth or gums while articulating the "you"s. Thus only the middle of the tongue moves.

Vibrato Demonstrations

Listen to my gross, inconsistent, and uncontrolled "you"s. You can hear that my first, slow, example involves a large, wobbly, pitch change, like a kid's slide whistle. In my second example I am moving my tongue less, and in a more controlled way, although after I take a breath my control deteriorates.

Check out Jason's amazingly fast and yet controlled vibrato. Each of his small pitch raises is the same as the others, and he is able to continue to vibrate the middle of his tongue in the consistent "you" motion *while* moving his entire tongue to produce different notes.

Ugo uses a combination of the tongue vibrato and the stomach vibrato, which I'll describe later. His tongue vibrato has less motion than Jason's, and thus is somewhat less dramatic.

I invented my adam's apple vibrato as an easy way to mimic a vibrato sound while I work on the real thing. I simply pinch a fold of the skin covering my adam's apple between thumb and forefinger, and shake it slightly as I whistle. It's better than nothing. Slightly.

Vibrato Practice

You can begin to practice your vibrato like this. Choose your most comfortable vibrato note to begin with, which will require some experimentation.

• Say some "you you you you you" articulations on that note, with tonguetip against lower front teeth. Move only the middle of the tongue, if possible. Work on making the same exact motion for each "you".

• See how little you can move the tongue and still hear a slight pitch change. The middle of your tongue should be moving only a fraction (1/4? 1/8?) of an inch. Try not to raise and drop your jaw.

• When you begin to hit sequences of a second or two of reasonably controlled "you"s at a time, begin trying to change pitch during the vibrato. While the middle of your tongue is making "you"s, your entire tongue must move forward or back to raise or lower the note. It's hard! Try it on just two notes.

• Then work your way up to a vibrato scale. At first, use a legato attack on the notes, without breaking up the airstream.

• Maintain a vibrato while starting the notes of a scale with a staccato attack. It may be easier to do this, at first, with puffs from the lungs rather than the harder attack using coughs from the epiglottis.

• Begin to integrate your developing vibrato into songs. Don't use (overuse) it on every note, just on notes that you want to emphasize (or, initially, on notes that seem convenient).

• Listen to the ways that the pros use vibrato. Whose vibrato do you prefer? Whose *utilization* of vibrato do you prefer?

Advanced Tone

When I discovered the warble, I realized that it would be half a year's work or more to even begin to master the complexities of this beautiful, versatile, liquid effect. Unfortunately, I had already committed myself to having this book done by fall of 1989, or I would have delayed it for a while, and devoted myself to an intensive course of "loodle"-ing.

Fortunately, I can provide you with some excellent examples from the masters, and then you can work on it yourself.

The Amazing Warble

The warble is obtained by using an articulation similar to the word "oodle" or "loodle" or "laydle" or "lodel". The "luh" articulation is an interesting and unique one, as it disrupts the airflow without stopping it. Most of our other articulations, like "tah", "dah", or "tuka", briefly close off the airstream. But when we articulate any "luh" sound, the tip of the tongue merely and momentarily divides the flow of air into parts that go around each side of the tonguetip.

When we say a "loodle" type articulation, the "dle" part is very different from our usual "dah". The "le" following the "d" softens it, so that as soon as the airstream has been blocked by the "d", it is then instantaneously opened but broken into two parts by the "le". The natural tendency appears to be for a note to go up slightly on the "dle" part of the articulation.

Types Of Warbles

The warble can be used in four main ways.

• As a single "loo" or a group of "loo"s (warbs, I call them), to emphasize single notes, almost as a type of mellow and liquid staccato attack.

• As a double tongued "oodle" or "loodle" or "laydle" or "lodel", to break each sound into two parts.

• As a triple tongued "loodle-oo", to break a sound into three parts.

• As a continuous warble, by saying "oodleloodleloodleloodle" for a delightful and very liquid **trill**.

Warble Demonstrations

Listen to me practice my "oodle"s, "loo"s, and "oodle-oos". Then listen to what it can *really* sound like.

Milton's demonstration uses a variety of effective tonal effects in a very short time. In the first line (four beats long) he mixes "loo"s and staccato notes without "loo"s (which I'll notate as "st"), in the order:

loo st loo loo loo st st

In his second line (also four beats), he uses "loodle"s, staccato notes, and a "loo" (as near as I can hear), like this:

st loodle loodle loodle loo st st

Roy mixes staccato notes with vibrato, "oodle"s and a continuous warble. He begins with four staccato notes ("Oh Danny boyyyy"), and swells into a vibrato on the fourth. He ends on a warbled trill. In between, notice how he uses some "oodle"s while he moves up and down on notes.

Jason's warble is very fast and regular, and thus may be called a trill, which the Harvard D. of M. defines as "consisting of the rapid alternation of a note with its upper neighbor". Notice that he tends not to shift notes *while* warbling, but instead connects the transition from one warbled note to a different one with a few in-between staccato notes.

Warble Work

• Say, without whistling, a lot of "loo"s, "oodle"s, "loodle"s, "ladle"s, "lodel"s, "loodle-oo"s, and "loodleloodleloodleloodle" articulations. Observe your tongue carefully.

• Practice, still without whistling, the alternation of the above articulations. Keep a steady beat while you do it. Also alternate the above with some staccato ("st") notes, which you can articulate either as puffs of air or as tiny soundless coughs. Can you do a repeated eight beat rhythm (breathing "br" on the eighth beat) like:

loo st loodle st loodle loodle loo br

• Choose a comfortable note, and say some "loo"s on it. You'll need to experiment to discover what notes are easiest to start doing this on.

• Now say the other warble articulations on that note. When you can say them all at least a little bit, try alternating them, or try the eight beat sequence that I gave you above.

• Now begin doing warbles on a variety of notes. When you can get some kind of warble on a few different notes, try maintaining a warble *while* raising or lowering the pitch from note to note, using a smooth legato attack.

• Listen to the ways in which the pros use warbling.

• Begin using "loo"s on a few notes, like the first notes of a major scale or the beginning of "Frere Jacques". The try a "loodle" on each note, then a "loodle-oo". This will seem impossible at first (you'll lose

the warble when you move your tongue). But in a few hours of practice you will be able to make small tone changes while warbling.

• When you're ready for a challenge, try some "loodle"s in a scale or a song, and hit one note on the "loo" and the next note on the "dle". This is a wonderful, liquid effect, and quite difficult!

Super Advanced Warble Work

When you can use the various warbles throughout your entire range (one of my favorite fantasies), try these:

• Use the eight beat "loodle" pattern above with a blues, minor, or major scale, using one beat of the articulation for each note of the scale (if you do a major or minor scale, you'll need to hit the last note instead of breathing — but if you're this advanced, you scarcely need to breathe anyway). Do this both going up and down.

• Do a major scale in which you articulate four "loodle"s, two notes to each "loodle", one on the "loo", the next on the "dle". Up and down, natch.

• Do the same thing with "loodle-loo"s, with one note on the "loodle", and the other on the "loo".

• Now begin to use these same techniques in songs.

• Experiment with the tongue position in the warble. If you lift more of your tongue towards the roof of your mouth for a "loo" or "loodle", the pitch will change more. What's most comfortable? (Probably what you've been doing already.) What sounds best to you?

• If you can hold your tongue in a tight "loo" position, and increase your volume, you may be able to produce a double tone, as my whistling friend Stu Woodward has begun to teach me to do. Try it, and let me know what happens — I'll put *you* in my next edition!

• Some of the pros occasionally use their **cheeks** to get a warble-like effect, but with much larger pitch jumps. Hit a tone with your cheeks held normally (close in), and then let first one, and then the other, fill with air and puff out. Does the tone change as each cheek fills? How much?

Slides

Listen to Jason sliiide! Practice sliding yourself, both up and down, or even down then up, or up then back down. Use vibrato, trill, or other effects while you slide, but concentrate on control of pitch and tone.

Legato slides in which each note of the scale is touched upon are called **glissandos**. This is the type of sound produced by a piano player sliding his or her fingernail continuously along the white keys.

Continuous slides without separate notes, like the slides of a trombone player, are called **portamentos.** So Jason's slide, which had no separate notes, would be a portamento, although many people use the terms interchangeably (if wrongly).

Stomach And Epiglottal Vibratos

The stomach vibrato (favored by harmonica players), involves tightening the abdominal muscles and "wavering" them on the exhale. Ugo uses this during his vibrato demonstration, combined with a throat vibrato.

Epiglottal vibratos are produced by making a smooth series of tiny coughs, like "uh-uh-uh-uh-uh". Practice these without the whistle, and see if you can do it continuously and soundlessly (or at least un-noisily). When done smoothly, constant air pressure is supplied by the lungs, and the epiglottis feels as though it is just rhythmically clapping over the entrance to the throat, rather like kids make a "Hollywood Indian" sound by clapping their hands over their mouths while saying "wooooo".

While listening to the recorded selections, you may be able to hear these effects used. The stomach vibrato has a very smooth sound, as Ugo demonstrates, and the throat vibrato usually has a slight cough sound underlying it.

Jason On His Tone

I often receive feedback about the size and resonance of my tone. The way I open up my sound is by projecting it from the entire inside of my head. I rarely think about my lips (except when they ache because I've been whistling too many big high pieces, or be-

cause I haven't sufficiently warmed up). Sometimes when I observe myself sending the tone from inside my head, I discover that I occasionally close my eyes and bend my head so that I'm literally projecting the sound out of the center of my forehead.

A comment that I frequently hear about my unmiked live indoor performances is that the sound does not seem to be coming from me. As I understand it, this is because the technique I use produces a resonant tone which vibrates the air in all corners of the room. It is this resonant tone, rather than just the stream of air moving between my lips, that people hear.

A Few Last Words On Tone

As Jason points out, there are many mental aspects to obtaining good tone. After working on the physical elements of relaxing and opening the throat, and learning the various effects, do some visualization work, as I have already discussed in the Pitch chapter (page 44). Virtually all professional singers do this type of work for their tone, no matter what terms (developing projection, a head register, presence) they use to describe the process.

Visualize yourself projecting great tone from your head or from your eyes, a tone that sets all the air around you into warm, open, liquid, vibration. Think of that warmness, and liquidity, as you whistle, and eventually it will translate itself into the physical reality of your improving tone.

Be aware also that there are environ- mental affects on tone. Some places have better acoustical properties than others. I love to whistle in bathrooms, stairwells, and tunnels, though of course in these public places it is important to be sensitive to your effect on other people's auditory space.

Ornamentation

Ornamentation means adding extra notes to the melody of a song. For example, instead of playing the usual melody notes of "Twinkle Twinkle Little Star" (first line), I add some extra neighboring notes of the scale to each original note (second line).

DO	DO	SO	SO	LA	LA	SO
Twin	kle	twin	kle	lit	tle	star

DO TI DO	SO fi SO	LA li LA	SO
Twin kle	twin kle	lit tle	star

For some excellent examples of this, check out Ugo's "House Of The Rising Sun" and Bob Larson's great *a cappella* (unaccompanied) version of the "Battle Hymn Of The Republic". By the way, *a cappella* whistling is the most demanding style, as there is not a guitar, piano, or orchestral backing (which can cover up a multitude of whistling sins, from breath noise to bad pitch).

Bird Whistling

The first whistler in the world was doubtless a caveperson imitating a bird. Since then, bird-style whistling has always been a popular category for pucker-ers everywhere. From the 1880's to the 1930's, a succession of bird-whistling performers fascinated Europe and America. The California School Of Artistic Whistling, started by Agnes Woodward in 1909, had branches all around the nation. This school taught whistling exclusively via a method based on learning bird calls. Marge Carlson, whose lovely "On Wings Of Song" is featured on the recording, is one of the world's foremost Woodward Method proponents.

At its simplest, bird whistling is based on using particular articulations in a variety of combinations, with a variety of notes. Listen to me demonstrate the "quitta", the "whit", and the "quitchaquia". But, as I said, rather than listening to *me* do this, listen to the experts.

Group Whistling

It's really fun to whistle *with* other people. There are lots of ways to do it, too. Two or more people can whistle exactly the same thing, which will produce a lovely full sound. But it's probably more exiting to have each person do something that complements the other. I love to whistle a blues or rock bass line, while the other person whistles lead solos. Then we switch, and I whistle lead while they provide the structure.

It's also very satisfying to whistle **rounds**. To do this, one person begins to whistle a song, and the other joins in after a given number of beats (often four). Listen to my example of a round version of "Frere Jacques" (I just happened to have a spot of extra room at the end of SoundSheet # 2-A).

When beginning to experiment with round whistling, it may be easier if you are both a little distance apart, so that you can each hear what you are doing best. If you hear the other person's whistling too loudly, it may confuse one or both of you, and you'll end up whistling the same thing at the same time, which rather defeats the purpose of rounds, if you think about it! "Row, Row, Row Your Boat" and "Three Blind Mice" are other good first choices for round whistling.

Part Three: The Rest

As I said in the "Preview" section: this part of the book contains whatever I couldn't seem to fit into Part One or Part Two, but couldn't bear to leave out, either. Chapters range from the practical "Pro Tips" to the metaphysical "Zen And The Art Of Whistling", and from the personal "How I Became The Voice Of Woodstock" to the multiple "The Best Whistlers In The World" to the universal (or should-be universal) "Whistling Etiquette". Skim, skip, or study, as you see fit. And enjoy!

The Best Whistlers In The World

I'm tremendously grateful to the six pro whistlers who, in addition to Jason, have contributed recorded selections for my instructional method. I would like to tell you a bit about each artist, their work, and other materials that they have available.

Milton Briggs:

Milton "Blue Mockingbird" Briggs, of Carmichael, California, doesn't just have great tone, pitch and rhythm. He is also the composer of virtually all his own material, and his own accompanist. The Grand Champion of the 1985 International Whistle-Off, Milton, 48, has been whistling since the age of four. His three octave range, from A to A, is the envy of many whistlers.

Notice his use of the warble articulations "oodle" and "oodle-oo" in both his upbeat major scale-based "Whistler's Polka" as well as his minor-based namesake composition "Blue Mockingbird" (in which selection you can hear the articulations especially clearly). Be aware also of his use of bird-style whistling at the end of "Blue Mockingbird".

A new composition, entitled "Opus in A minor" will be out on cassette soon. Milton is sometimes available for performances and fund-raising concerts. For a cassette of his work (including uncut versions of the two songs excerpted here), send $10.00 plus $2.00 postage and handling to: 2516 Winsford Lane, Box WP, Carmichael, CA 95608.

Marge Carlson

As I've already mentioned, Marge is one of the world's leading experts on the Agnes Woodward bird-based style of whistling. But this doesn't mean that she "just" does bird calls. Rather, she uses her ability to create bird sounds in two ways. She uses recorded overdubs of her bird calls as a background for the melody of Mendelsohn's "On Wings Of Song", and then, within the context of the song, she also uses avian effects to advance the melody.

Marge is now involved in a fascinating project: using whistling to speed the growth rate of plants. The theory behind this project is based on studies indicating that the vibrational ranges present in the song of birds help to open the nutrient intake organs in the cells of plants. By using a spray-on nutrient while playing a specially recorded tape of Marge's whistling, the Sonic Bloom Company (708 109th Lane NE, Blaine, MN 55434) claims increased nutrient intake rates of up to 700 times normal!

Marge's two cassette tapes, "On Wings Of Song" and "The Sweetest Song", are available for $10.00 each plus $2.00 postage and handling. Send check or request for performance information to: Artistry In Whistling, 2448 East Balfour Ave. Box WP, Fullerton, CA 92631.

Jason Serinus

Jason's dramatic and distinctive sound is characterized by his very high range, almost continuous vibrato, and mostly legato rather than staccato attack. Jason's music is very emotional, full of sweeps and dynamic changes. In person, as perhaps you can tell from his photographs, Jason is a lively and expressive performer.

Notice his lovely vibrato in Stephen Foster's "Jeannie With The Light Brown Hair". In Verdi's "Ernani, Involami", he uses lots of warble with vibrato, and long, swooping portamentos. His accompanist is Lloyd Carroll.

If you would like to hear more, his cassette tape, "Jason Serinus Whistler Extraordinaire", is available only by mail. Including 16 classical and contemporary pieces, this professionally recorded tape is real-time copied with Dolby B noise reduction for optimal sound quality. To order, send $10.00 (CA residents please add 7% sales tax) plus $2.00 postage and handling to Jason Serinus, P.O. Box 3073-WP, Oakland, CA. 94609. Please allow up to 6 weeks for delivery.

Dr. Ugo Conti

Ugo is a physicist, and inventor of the Conti-1 and Conti-2 whistle synthesizers. He is one of the nation's top classical whistlers, having taken top honors at both the International Whistle-Off and the National Whistlers Convention. As with most classical whistlers, he places great emphasis on fast, clear, staccato notes.

Notice his ornamentation in "The House Of The Rising Sun", in which he accompanies himself on guitar. He uses both the blues and the minor scales to improvise and ornament with, especially on the second verse.

In his second piece, "Synthesizer Dandy", Ugo begins by just solo whistling into the microphone of the Conti-1 Synthesizer. He then uses his fingers on the control levers to manipulate the tone generated by his whistle. This piece was done live, with no overdubs — just him whistling into his machine. Ugo's generous gesture at the last Whistle-Off (he gave his First Place Classical trophy to Sean Lomax, whom he thought deserved better than Second Place) will be remembered by all in attendance as a remarkable display of good sportspersonship. The Conti-1 is available for $2795, and the smaller Conti-2 for $475 (both MIDI compatible). Inquiries may be addressed to: EMI, PO Box 463-WP, El Cerrito, CA 94530-0463

Roy Thoreson

From the town of Calgary in Canada, Roy is the world's only multiple (four time) winner of the International Whistle-Off. Just a bare minute of listening to his lovely rendition of "Greensleeves", and you'll see why!

Roy's inventive use of rhythm adds a jazzy feeling to this classic piece. He uses a hint of reverb on this delightful recording, although unfortunately there are a few noises on the tape, perhaps caused by sleeve buttons hitting the accompanying guitar. At the end of each verse (during the time that would be occupied by the word "Greensleeves"), he does a fantastic combination warble, consisting of a tiny bit of fast warble, then two or three slow, clear "loodle"s, then an extended fast warble — three seconds of heaven!

Roy, 57, has a two-and-a-half octave usable range, and performs all around Canada. His cassette tape is available for $10.00 plus $4.00 postage and handling ($2.00 for Canadians) to: 7323 Silver Springs Rd. NW, Box WP, Calgary, Alberta, Canada T3B 3X1

Note: Observant mail order customers will notice the addition of a suspicious "Box WP" to each of the above addresses. All monies go directly to the artists, and Musical I Press gets no cut. But we would like the whistlers to be able to tell how interested parties have heard of them, so please use the "Box WP" when ordering cassettes.

Dr. Jack Cohen

Jack, of Montreal, Canada, plays some of the most difficult classical music that a whistler can: long violin pieces with lots of fast notes. He has a two octave range on fast pieces, two-and-a-half on slow ones, and puts a great deal of energy into improving his breath by jogging and by whistling especially long passages. Jack has often been the featured soloist with the McGill University Chamber Orchestra and the Hamilton, Ontario Philharmonic Symphony. Since 1983, he has been working with the accompanist featured on the recording, classical guitarist Davis Joachim.

Since he uses few tone effects other than a subtle vibrato, his lovely clear tone, excellent pitch, and accurate staccato passages must carry his part in their rendition of Purcell's "Strike The Viol". His cassette tape is available for $10.00 plus $4.00 postage and handling ($2.00 for Canadians) to: 5885 Cote Des Neiges Road, Suite 600-WP, Montreal, Canada H3S 2T2

Bob Larson

Minneapolis-based Bob, 64, has been whistling for as long as he can remember, and performing since the age of seven. Grand Champion of the 1986 International Whistle-Off, he plays throughout the midwest, accompanying himself with autoharp and a rich Burl Ives-like voice.

The only *a cappella* piece featured on my recording, his "Battle Hymn Of The Republic" showcases his use of the warble as a means of getting from one note to another, as well as his skill in jazzing up a major scale-based piece with articulated rhythms and extra notes added from the blues scale.

Bob's two cassettes, with 25 songs each, are available for $10.00 each plus $2.00 postage and handling from: 3201 North Bryant Avenue Box WP, Minneapolis, MN 55412

"The Whistling Voice Of Woodstock"

To tell you the truth, I have no idea how I became "The Voice of Woodstock." I mean, I know what I did, and who called who, and what seemed to have transpired. But how I managed to be in the right place in the right time has to do with a guiding energy that is much bigger than my little birdbrain can begin to comprehend.

It began, of all places, in Hollywood. (Have you heard that line before?) I remember learning of an audition for a Hollywood TV show called "America Votes for Tomorrow's Stars". Shortly thereafter, in the spring of 1978, never having been to Hollywood before and knowing nothing about what I was supposed to do, I found myself auditioning in front of an audience of big name Hollywood people. They loved my whistling / mime combination as I performed "It's Only a Paper Moon" (my debut piece on The Tonight Show a year later), but had no idea what to do with me when I whistled Puccini's "Entrance of Butterfly" from the opera "Madame Butterfly". Unable to pigeonhole me into a marketable category, they sent me home, starless.

On the plane I met Judy Berlin, a coach for child actors and actresses. When I whistled for her in the airplane parking lot, she said, "You should whistle the voice of a character in a children's cartoon. You should contact Lee Mendelson."

Three months later, I finally got it together to call up Judy and ask how I could find Lee Mendelson. When she told me that his offices were in Burlingame, CA, about 45 minutes and numerous social classes away from my starving artist "two small rooms-behind-a-store for $76/month including utilities" apartment, I called him on the phone. All I knew was that he had something to do with children's cartoons. Taking a deep breath, I gave him my non-stop rap about being an artist and whistling with symphony orchestras. He gave me a polite nod, told me to send him a letter and a tape if I had one, and promptly hung up the phone. I shuffled off to my typewriter, whipped out a cover letter, assembled all the articles, resumes and demo tapes I could find, and sent them off to him.

Some months later, I returned home to find the little red light on my answering machine beckoning to me. This was the period when I prayed that every ring might be a call from Hollywood. Eagerly I rewound the tape to play back something like the following:

"Hello, Jason Serinus? This is Lee Mendelson. Look, Charles Schulz and I were thinking about using you as the voice of the bird Woodstock in a Peanuts cartoon. Do you know "O Mio Babbino Caro" by Puccini? If so, could you send us a tape?"

My mind swooned. "Charles Schulz? Woodstock? Peanuts? You mean Lee Mendelson works with Charles Schulz? Oh my God. I've been performing "O Mio Babbino Caro" for the last 2 years. It's my favorite

operatic aria. I don't believe this. This just can't be real!"

Needless to say, within half an hour I had phoned up Lee Mendelson and begun setting up my primitive recording equipment. My little recorder played the orchestral accompaniment as I whistled into the mike I had hung over a hot water pipe. Three (or was it thirty three?) takes later, something passable enough to send to Lee Mendelson had been recorded. He and Charles Schulz thought it "sensational," and they called me to say I was in.

It took at least 6 months more until I finally recorded the aria. It felt like an eternity, and I many times feared the whole thing was not going to happen. Happily, in the intervening period I began to perform regularly at San Francisco's Fisherman's Wharf and Pier 39, and became a much better whistler. By the time the recording day actually approached, I was ready.

But not quite. I entered the recording space filled with fear and suffering from a psychosomatic cold. Happily, musical director Ed Bogas knew some acupressure and massage, and got some breath moving through my frozen frame. Ed's brother Roy played the electric piano, and I began to whistle. Although I thought my whistling was less than perfect (I always do, to tell you the truth), Charles Schulz, or "Sparky", as everyone calls him, loved one of the first takes. Thank goodness, because my nerves could not have lasted very long.

For those of you who have never seen the Peanuts cartoon, the plot of "She's a

Good Skate, Charlie Brown" revolves around an ice skating competition. Just as the heroine, Peppermint Patty, is about to compete, her tape recorded accompaniment fails. But little yellow Woodstock walks up to the skating rink's microphone and puts it to his lips — and Woodstock is indeed the only bird that has lips — and begins to whistle Peppermint Patty's music. You can guess what happens next.

The actual recording session of me whistling Woodstock's aria was shot by a film crew. It was used in an award-winning story that PM Magazine ran about how I became "The Whistling Voice of Woodstock." I believe that Charles Schulz was watching it when he began to animate the scene of Woodstock whistling the music, so that he could see how I breathed, and how I held my body and mouth.

Several years after the cartoon's debut in February 1980, I was asked to record a different original piece for the storybook / audio cassette version of the cartoon. Not too long after that, the video of "She's a Good Skate, Charlie Brown" was released with the original version of Woodstock's aria .

Whistling Woodstock's voice has been the answer to a long-held dream. I have always wanted to share my song with the world, and Charles Schulz has made it possible. It has been an incredible opportunity, and a great joy!

It is my hope that this book, and the record contained within it, can help you to find such musical joy within yourself.

On Musicianship

This chapter will give you some advice on how to take whatever whistling skills you have and use them to make music. In the 18th century, an important trend in Italian vocal music was called the *bel canto* (beautiful song) school. In this style of singing, beauty of sound and brilliancy of performance were emphasized over the emotional content of the piece. Jason and I believe the reverse: that feeling for a piece of music takes precedence over technical virtuosity. And now I'll let Jason express himself on this subject, one on which, as a great dramatic interpreter of music, he is well qualified to speak.

Expression

If you listen carefully to any great singer or instrumentalist, be they classical or country, jazz or New Age, soprano or saxophonist, you will find that their tone and manner of expression perfectly suit their music. Heavy metal musicians will be loud and driving, with both voice and instruments having a sharp edge. Country western singers will often have a melancholy sound to their voice, or have that particular quality which produces the feeling that they're singing "just like the folks back home." Classical singers will on some occasions employ a very rich and full sound, and at other times pare down to a thin sweet column. Tone and manner of expression chosen all depend on what the artist wants to convey, and how the artist wants his or her listeners to feel.

As I moved from whistling opera in a little San Francisco neighborhood bar to being heard internationally via television, audio and videotape, I discovered that all the cliches I heard over and over again about how "happy whistlers" always "whistle a happy tune" had basically left people unprepared for an art that in many ways can parallel the expressive power and range of the human voice. This "happy" myth had limited people's imagination about the artistic potential of whistling, and diminished their expectations of what they themselves could express as whistlers.

Don't get me wrong. I love whistling a happy tune. Pieces like "On the Sunny Side of the Street, " "The Italian Street Song," and "Singin' in the Rain" are a joy to perform, and express a lot of who I am. But, like yourself, I experience grief as well as joy. I have deep feelings of love, sadness, loyalty, longing, trust, and belief in God. And I have a deep desire to create harmony in my own life and on the planet. If I have chosen whistling to be my musical medium of expression, I want it to voice all of me, and to be true to what I am feeling. It does not satisfy me creatively to simply voice the part of me that I am expected to voice. And I certainly do not want other people to be limited in their expression. So please don't think that you need to limit yourself to any type or style of music.

Selecting Your Repertoire

To be a good whistler, you need to listen to a piece of music and understand it, even before you begin to whistle it. Ask yourself some questions: How does it make you feel? Is there one predominant emotion? If so, can you convey that in your whistling? If one part of it is sad, and the other part more upbeat, would you like to emphasize both aspects, or mainly concentrate on one? If both, when should you make the emotional transition? Underlying these questions is a deeper issue: Is such a piece suitable for you, or does it call for more than you can give it?

You also need to listen to yourself whistling it. Here you have a tremendous advantage over the whistlers of the past, because for a relatively small investment you can buy a decent cassette recorder and external mike that can play back to you a fair approximation of how you sound to others. You can begin to hear your whistling strengths, and eventually, after much experimentation (and keeping an open mind), develop a sense of what kind of music you do best. Or, conversely, you can decide what kind of music you want to express yourself with, and then develop the techniques necessary to perform it.

When I began to whistle at age 11, I did not have the advantage of a tape recorder. What I did have were recordings of some of the great operatic singers of the century. As I listened to their records, I marveled at how magnificently they could mold the human voice into a rich, vibrant and full instrument. Because the music they were singing spoke to what I was feeling in my heart, I began to whistle along. The more I listened and whistled, the more my imagination and my whistling began to grow.

As I heard more great opera singers, I realized how distinctive each singer's voice was, and how different they sounded in different pieces. In fact, I was so overwhelmed by their artistry that when I first began performing before the public, I was always trying to match my whistling voice with the voice on the record playing in my head. It was not until I began to work with my teacher that I realized that I too had a unique "voice", and that I needed to focus on developing my own manner of expression, rather than on duplicating someone else's.

In retrospect, I realize that intention and imagination are essential ingredients of good whistling. And somewhere in the process of listening and imitating, I began to develop a clear intention of what I was trying to accomplish. My imagination being rather unbridled, I never stopped to think that maybe as a whistler I could not sing in the same way as the people whose voices excited me. I knew what I was trying to say — what feelings I wanted to convey — and I began to develop ways to mold my voice to the feelings that were moving through my heart.

I cannot teach you how to do this for yourself. I can give you pointers, but I cannot lead the way. Your imagination, your willingness to listen, and your willingness to explore the range of what you can do will determine how your whistling will develop. Even without a teacher, you'll know when you're on the right track, because people will sit up and take notice.

Learning A New Piece

When I choose my repertoire, I try to be realistic about what I can reasonably pull off. Even though I prefer to whistle classical and popular vocal music, I do not have the singer's advantage of being able to use the language itself to add expression to the music. So I look for music in which the movement of the notes themselves is enough to compensate for this deficiency — music with lots of variation in pitch, dynamics, and rhythm.

I also attempt to understand where my strengths lie. When I find a piece that feels and sounds right to me, I spend a while exploring it. Depending upon the range of the pitches, it may take a while for me to place it properly in my mouth and throat, to decide what note to start on, and when to change octaves if necessary. I need time to learn how much air I need to inhale to whistle each of its phrases with integrity, and to connect one phrase with another so that the piece flows from beginning to end. I must discover how much breath I need to allow that long high note at the end to float in the air with seemingly effortlessness, and to last as long as I want. I then have to plan to take that breath at a point where it will have the least effect on the flow of the music.

I learn when to raise and lower my volume, and how I can make one phrase follow the next so that the piece stands as a whole. Finally, I perform it enough times so that I gain the confidence that allows me to whistle it to others without holding my breath in fear.

I know of no finer way to open your mind to the myriad range of expression available to a whistler than to encourage you to listen to the masters and to attend local and national whistling competitions. When you hear someone that you like, you will discover how all the elements I discuss above can be brought together into coherent and delightful musical expression. And as you continue to practice, you will discover how much you too can do when, as Lauren Bacall told Humphrey Bogart in "To Have And Have Not", you just "put your lips together and blow".

Pro Tips

Here are just a few of the issues that professional whistlers deal with. But the best way to learn the ins and outs of the trade is to come to one of the annual competitions or conventions, so don't forget to read the sections on the International Whistle-Off and the National Whistlers Convention.

Microphone Technique

Any number of microphones may be used to record or amplify a whistler, from the $4.00 Radio Shack variety to a thousand dollar studio rig. Omni-directional mics (which pick up sound from all directions) are preferred to uni-directional ones (which pick up sound from only one direction), and the cardioid mic (an omni-directional mic that picks up sound best in a heart-shaped area) is the most popular omni. But perhaps most important is placement of the mic in relation to the lips.

There is generally a spot a few inches away from the lips and slightly off-center that will give you the best results with the least mouth noise. But the only way to find this spot is through experimentation. It may be easier for someone else to listen while you move the mic around, since you will be hearing the whistle inside your head in addition to the sound from the amplifier.

Some whistlers, like Jason, prefer to hold the mic by hand, which allows for greater freedom of movement on stage, but makes it harder to maintain a consistent position of mic to lips. Others find that holding a mic for long periods of time is stressful to their hand, arm, or shoulder, and use an adjustable mic stand.

Monitor Technique

Monitoring refers to the act of listening to yourself whistle or to your accompaniment while performing. When playing solo or with acoustic accompaniment, monitoring will most likely be unnecessary. But if you're playing with a band, it may be hard to hear yourself, and you will either need headphones (my preference) or a small amplifier (also called a monitor, Jason's preference) placed directly in front of you. There are few things worse than being in front of a big audience and not being able to hear yourself, so make sure that you'll have a monitor if you think you may need one!

On Stage Fright

Some have it, some don't. But I think that stage fright can be a good thing, since there are only two useful ways to deal with it, both of them with eminently beneficial side effects.

You can try to overcome it by learning how to deal with your own mind, since stage fright is just another category of irrational fear, and irrational fear is simply one of the things that undisciplined minds tend to indulge in. I have letters from a number of people who are using my meditation methods (as propounded in the books *The Three*

Minute Meditator and *MetaPhysical Fitness*, see my Sales Pitch) to deal with performance anxiety. Even a few moments practice of the breathing meditation (page 38) before a show may be of use. I believe that any good method of meditation, diligently applied, will help cope with fears of any sort. So if whistling stage fright gives you a reason to take up the time-honored art of meditation, you can't lose.

The other option is to let your fear of stage fright *motivate* you to prepare for a performance to the absolute best of your ability. And since that's something that you should be doing anyway, well, once again, you just can't lose! Here are some pro tips on preparation.

How Jason Prepares To Perform

Practice is the cornerstone of a good performance. You must know not only the notes of a piece of music, but exactly what you need to put into it, energy-wise and breath-wise, to make it "sing."

Knowledge of your music, however, is only the first step. The foundation of confidence, in my opinion, lies in:

• *knowing exactly what you are capable of giving in a performance, and being practiced and prepared to give it*

• *knowing what you need in terms of preparation and warm-up time to be able to deliver your best*

• *making sure you take the time to do whatever is necessary for optimal performance.*

When I perform, I make sure that whoever is sponsoring my performance knows exactly what my needs are. I let them know about my accompaniment, miking and monitor requirements, and my need to warm up and relax in a quiet space before I go on. Whenever possible, I meditate, do yoga, and swim before performing.

I arrive at the performance sufficiently ahead of time to allow for everything to flow smoothly. Even if my sponsors have a tape recorder, I bring my own to replace theirs in case I discover that it wobbles or is pitched incorrectly. Because I prefer not to drink tap water, or water that is iced, I either bring my filtered water along or request that my sponsors have some available for me both on-stage and in the warm-up area.

Like any athlete or singer, I always warm up before I whistle. While I have no problem whistling "Happy Birthday" on a moment's notice, I cannot whistle large range operatic pieces without first limbering up my instrument. To produce free high notes demands a lot of cooperation from a lot of muscles — muscles which in peak form can give the illusion of doing next to nothing. My sound, frankly, can be edgy and forced if my breath and muscles are not operating perfectly. Truthfully, my highest notes may not be there the way I want them (or there at all) until 20 minutes into my warm-up.

If I learn that there is no space available to warm up, I warm up beforehand by whistling my brains out in my car as I travel. I bring my Walkperson, headphones, plastic glass, and water bottle with the handle along, so that if necessary I can walk around the block or even retreat to the Men's Room to complete my warm-up before it is my time to go on. Whether I am performing for 3 minutes or 90, I make sure that by the time I appear in front of an audience, I am ready to give them my all.

I also watch my diet before I perform. I once ate such a big meal that I couldn't take in deep breaths. I never did that again! I also make sure that I don't eat salty or highly spiced foods, which seem to affect my whistling. It may be totally different for you. I don't eat dairy foods, but know some whistlers who must avoid them before performing. If I'm performing in a place that will not have food that I can eat, I bring my own along. Frankly, I'd rather have a little rumbling in my stomach than a sour note in my whistling.

Jason's Secrets

I'll let you in on a personal whistling secret. I find that a slightly oily coating in my mouth is conducive to optimal performing. Sometimes I bring along my old mouth-preparation standby, oil-roasted cashews. By slowly and completely chewing a small package of these addictive morsels, I can coat my mouth sufficiently with the oil to insure that my notes flow through freely. I have even on occasion brought along a little squeeze bottle of oil, or run out to the convenience store for a small bottle of olive oil. This may sound fussy or neurotic to some (but who cares?). The point is, when I know that I have prepared myself in the best ways that

I know how, I know that I am ready to go onstage without fear.

I rarely begin my show with an extremely difficult piece of music. Rather, I choose something that lies within my most comfortable range and which promises to give me and my listeners true delight. This gives me a chance to relax into the acoustics and the energy of a listener-filled space, and to "tune myself" to the people and the room. If I'm nervous, this onstage opening piece gives me a chance to whistle those nerves away. If I discover that my whistling isn't flowing as well as I would like, I pace the rest of my program accordingly. I would rather put off my most technically difficult pieces until late in the program than to approach them with fear in the beginning. On the other hand, my encore selections are chosen to please an audience but not to be the most demanding pieces in my repertoire.

And that's both the end of my performance, and the end of this performance, for me. I hope that you enjoyed my recorded pieces, and I'll see you on stage!

Whistling Etiquette

The title of this book is not just "How To Whistle Like A Pro". It continues on to say, "without driving anyone else crazy". As I said in the beginning of the book, *anything* can be abused. From dieting to overeating, indulgence to abstinence, sports to spirituality, soup to nuts — anything done without conscious awareness can ultimately have a negative effect on ourselves and the others around us.

Conversely, if we maintain a high sense of awareness, of, once again, both ourselves and those around us, anything, indeed, everything that we do can have a positive effect.

We can annoy a passer-by with our whistling, or brighten someone's day. We can vex our families and co-workers, or entertain them. We can whistle out of habit as a compulsive custom, or do it out of joy as a means of sincere self-expression.

Whistling Self-Awareness

By making an earnest study of whistling, you have taken the first step towards whistling awareness. The exercises and instruction in this book, coupled with the examples set by the great whistlers, will help you to take your own growing musical abilities seriously. This will help you try to be *musical* whenever you whistle, rather than just diverting yourself. This doesn't mean that you must be grave or critical whenever you whistle — more the opposite.

It just means that you should learn to *appreciate* the opportunity to make a joyful noise, to do it with joy, with gratitude, with awareness.

Whistling Sensitivity To Others

The Native Americans had an oft-quoted motto: Walk A Mile In The Other Person's Moccasins. By trying to see a situation from the other's view as well as our own, we gain invaluable perspective. For instance, when we do not yet whistle too well, we gain much more pleasure from the act than do our listeners. So we have to be especially careful not to impose our sound on someone else's space.

The concept of auditory space is one which has yet to be exhaustively defined. There are certain places in which sound, by law or custom, is restrained. It's as clear as black and white that only a person looking to annoy would whistle in the library, or in church. But whistling late at night while walking in a populated area, be it urban or suburban, is a grayer zone. You are awake (I assume you are, if you're whistling). But others may not be. Although you are in transit, you may leave a line of awakened early risers in your whistling wake. You've only bugged each one for a moment, it's true. But that's no excuse. With a bit of reflection, you become aware that if *you* were on the edge of sleep, and someone passed by making any kind of sound, it would disturb you. So you refrain from whistling on the street after a certain hour.

And that hour might be different in the downtown nightlife district than it would be in a more rural zone.

Confined Spaces

I think that the benefit of the doubt must always be applied to situations involving confined spaces. To put it simply: either When In Doubt, Ask — or When In Doubt, Don't! (Whistle). This doesn't mean that you just automatically don't whistle in your cousin's Volkswagen bug on a cross-country trip. It means that you realize that it is *your* responsibility to be constantly aware of whether you are disturbing anyone.

Confined spaces aren't always physical in nature — they can be temporal, or time-based, as well. The whistling neighbor in Dear Abby's column probably had the mistaken impression that because he was on his own property, and outside, that he could whistle as he pleased (he also, in the newspaper, sounded like a compulsive and continual whistler rather than a conscious one). Yet because he was in more or less permanent proximity to someone else, it was his responsibility to make sure that he was not bothering them. People working together, housemates, and relatives fall into this same category.

Different people have vastly different feelings about their auditory space. Some are protective, others completely casual. But if you take responsibility for being aware of how others are reacting to your sound, you can adjust your behaviour accordingly.

You may have to let go of taking their response to your whistling personally. There are people who want to hear nothing. There are people who hate to see or hear anyone else enjoying themselves. There are people who will enjoy asking you to stop, because it gives them a feeling of power or control. However, if someone wishes you to stop, whether they've asked you or whether you've just made yourself aware of their feelings, it's not a reflection on you or your music. It's a reflection on them, on the situation, on the fact that they had an argument with their spouse that morning, or a headache. So let go of any negative feelings that you may have, go someplace private (inside your own car is always a safe place), and whistle up a storm!

Even when you're asked to whistle, or told that it's okay to do so, maintain your awareness of your listeners' feelings. Because as Johann Joachim Quantz, flute teacher to Frederick The Great, said in 1752, a person should not play too much, "lest we must beg him as many times to cease as we had to beg him to begin..."

Zen And The Art Of Whistling

Perhaps it does seem like a strange title – but it's not a joke. Because the psychological principles that underlie Zen and similar disciplines have recently been used to teach subjects as diverse as sports and drawing. Millions of people have learned new skills from books like "Inner Tennis", "Inner Skiing" and "Drawing on the Right Side of the Brain". And this same type of approach is well-suited for the teaching of music, and especially for the teaching of a musical pursuit as intuitive as whistling!

The serious practitioners of Zen, Karate, Aikido, and Yoga often seem to possess nearly superhuman abilities. The best Zen archers can send an arrow straight to the target while blindfolded, the Karate and Aikido Masters can disarm a dozen simultaneous attackers, and the top-of-the-line Yogis can voluntarily suspend pulse and respiration. The adept students of more "Western" disciplines like self-hypnosis and "superlearning" often perform the slightly less herculean tasks of quitting smoking or learning 1500 words of a foreign language in a single day. But what have these strange yet impressive feats to do with whistlers?

A Martial Arts Analogy

The student of Karate engages in two very different main types of training.

• On the technical level, he or she practices specific punches, kicks and blocks until they feel comfortable, natural and familiar.

• On the mental level, He or she will also practice a mental state known as "one-pointedness". In this state the student is relaxed but totally focused on the attacker, so that whichever offensive or defensive move is needed will flow naturally without mental analysis or self-criticism.

Clearly, to criticize or analyze oneself in the midst of battle ("I should have kicked his kneecap, and then...") would distract concentration from the crucial present situation. Zen and the other disciplines mentioned above also use approximately the same "two-way" teachings to achieve their results (although the words used to label such teachings differ widely).

Let The Music Flow

Learning the ability to make music requires similar preparation. We must learn the rules and guidelines of music theory, and then practice technical skills, rhythm patterns, scales, and tonal effects, starting with the simple and building up to the complex. At the same time, in order to learn to allow the music to flow freely from our hearts and mouths, we'll have to begin to locate that mental state which blues and jazz musicians refer to as *playing from the gut* or *playing with soul*.

It's hard to describe that mental place in words. Some would say it's like being on *automatic pilot* after you've learned to drive well, as I discussed in my clutch analogy. Others might say it's like the state you're in when you've danced so freely and wildly (perhaps after drinking a few beers) that for just a few minutes you forgot to notice whether you were embarrassing your partner or not! A psycho-physiologist would probably prefer to label this place as the *right hemisphere* of the brain. A martial artist would call it the *hara* or *one-point*, and a hypnotist the *self-induced trance*. The Zen monk might know such a space as *mushin* or *no-mind*.

Regardless of the terminology used to describe it, this "musical flow state" is clearly related to the way in which we can often begin a sentence without thinking and the words just flow out, unplanned yet mostly making sense.

How To Do It

You've already been practicing the technical side of the process, in your study of music theory, rhythm, breathing, pitch, and tone. And that's good, because the more familiar and comfortable you are with the technical and physical side of playing, the more options you will have at your disposal when you put your brain on automatic pilot and just play from your soul!

If you tend to be perfectionistic or hard on yourself, your most important mental task will be to allow yourself some freedom from self-criticism as you explore my book and recording. Focus and concentrate on my written words, my voice, and the music. Don't permit those nagging, self-hating inner messages ("You can't do this, you're tone-deaf" or "You didn't understand that part right away? You must be dumb") to distract you. Give 'em the day off! Most of my instructions are quite simple, and easily understood if you read or listen to them as many times as you need to, without "self-sabotage"!

The "Master" Mental Exercises

Once you've declared at least a brief moratorium on self-criticism, you'll be ready to use the mental teaching techniques that I've integrated into the text. The most important ones are the Breath Meditation (on page 38) and the visualization exercise explained in the Mental Training section of the Pitch chapter (page 44). These two exercises can be used to prepare for *any* of the other exercises in this book, if used as followed. In fact, these two "master" exercises can be used to help you accomplish *anything* in life, musical or not!

Spend one or two minutes doing the Breathe Meditation, to put you into a relaxed and clear-minded mood. Then use the visualization exercise to focus on whatever you wish to accomplish. Don't just picture yourself enjoying the final *rewards* of your wish, but try to envision yourself patiently and competently performing every step necessary to *reach* that reward. Then begin the actual exercise, be it a breathing, a range increasing, or a tone exercise.

Use a quick run-through of the two master exercises (even a few seconds of each will help) before performing music as well for yourself on the street or for an audience at a concert. Preparing in this way will help you to take yourself and your whistling seriously, as I discuss in the Whistling Self-Awareness section of the Etiquette chapter.

Seems kind of hard to believe? New age-ey, perhaps? Yet even if you are a hard-headed, skeptical, non-believer in such "mystical" pursuits, these mental teaching techniques will work for you if you do them... whether you believe in them or not.

The Scale Of The Universe

Many people consider music to be just a pleasant diversion or at most a popular art form. Yet the form and structure of music appear to be reflections of the entire universe, from atom to galaxy.

As I explained in the music theory chapter, the ancient Greeks used ratio theory with great success in many different disciplines. But Pythagoras was not merely grinding his favorite theoretical axe when he applied mathematical ratios to the distances between notes. I say this because the musical notes that he obtained and the ratios that he used to produce them have a far, far wider application than he knew (or *did* he?).

Strangely enough, even though other cultures have scales of vastly varying size and complexity (the Chinese scale has five notes and the East Indian scale twenty two), many of the notes used in *all* cultures are the same. It's possible that this amazingly widespread usage of certain notes is due "only" to the psychological and physical properties that all human beings have in common. But this explanation, based as it is on the *human* experience, cannot begin to explain why Pythagoras' ratio itself (not just the notes) appears to possess an awesome universality. For it seems that both the ratio of the distances between the sun and the planets of the solar system, and the ratio of the distances between the quantum levels of energy in the molecule, bear a strong similarity to — you guessed it — the ratios used by Pythagoras in determining scale structure.

Perhaps we human beings are just unlucky enough to be the wrong *size* to appreciate the flabbergastingly high degree of order in all creation — too big to appreciate the sub-atomic, and too small to appreciate the cosmic. But, luckily, we *are* exactly the right size to appreciate the joyful noise of our own pucker-and-blow. And we begin to realize that by looking deeply enough and gratefully enough into *anything*, even the simple act of whistling, we find that we can learn something about *everything*.

Our gratitude and awe reach a crescendo when we understand that the scales upon which our music is based are representative of the entire well-integrated unity of the universe!

Teaching Kids

As I said in my section on pre-whistling encouragement, young children appear to have an inborn ability to mimic vocal sounds. My own eight month old daughter, Katie, can do a far better "Spanish R" than I can, as well as an uncannily accurate reproduction of the horrible throat-clearing noise that I make in the morning. For the past month she has been puckering her lips and blowing, in mimicry of my preparations for this project. My wife makes the claim that Katie once briefly produced a weak whistle, but alas, I wasn't there at the time, so it remains hearsay and therefore not scientifically admissable evidence.

While researching this book, I encountered numerous anecdotes of children under a year old who spontaneously learned to whistle. Most of the people relating these anecdotes felt that the children were mimicking birds. So it seems that simply exposing young children to the sound of whistling may be enough to teach them to do it.

If a child is old enough to follow verbal instructions, you can help them learn to whistle in the following way (even if you can't whistle, yet).

• Help them to do the mouth exploration exercises.

• Make sure that they can keep their nose closed (like blowing out birthday candles).

• Show them the pucker picture on page 19, and explain to them how to pout out their lips in a slight "fishface" (kids love that silly stuff).

• Practice blowing over the bottle.

• Have them listen to the recording — lots!

• Once they begin to get a whistle, use the "For Real Beginners" section in the Pitch chapter. Most kids can get "Frere Jacques", "Three Blind Mice", and the simplified "Mary Had A Little Lamb" pretty quickly!

• After they've gotten this far, they can work on any other song, or any other part of this book. Try whistling with them in rounds, as described at the end of the Tone chapter. Soon they'll be out-whistling you!

Two last comments. Keep in mind that, for young boys especially, whistling may be mentally tied to feelings about masculinity. It can be painful for a boy not to be able to whistle if most of his friends can. So be sensitive, and *never* laugh at his attempts. Some girls may have gotten the sadly erroneous idea that women shouldn't whistle. This can be dispelled by having them listen to Marge Carlson's recording, and by informing them that Nancy Foran, of Yakima, Washington, was the 1981 Grand Champion of the International Whistle-Off competition...

International Association Of Whistlers

The International Association of Whistlers was formed in the fall of 1983, during the International Whistle-Off. Its goals are:

- to provide a means of communication for all whistlers and those who enjoy whistling
- To encourage and promote whistling performances as an entertainment medium
- To encourage participation in competitive whistling events, and
- To be a centralized resource for whistling information

The IAW newsletter, **Whistlers' Notes**, is an entertaining and informative compendium of hints, events, letters from pro and amateur whistlers, controversy, gossip, and tips on competing at the various whistling competitions. Editor Mimi Drummond is a highly ranked competitive whistler with a sharp ear for whistling news!

To join the IAW and receive the newsletter, send a check ($25.00 for the first year, $10.00 for each additional year, non-whistlers only $10.00 for the first year) to: IAW, 590 Lamplighter Road, Horsham, PA 19044.

IAW president Carole Kass, of Shaker Heights, Ohio, is also a serious competitive whistler. During a long conversation about this book, she brought up a subtle (it must have been subtle, since I had never explicitly thought of it) point that I feel is very well worth mentioning. Carole pointed out that whistlers can be divided into two categories, those who are influenced and inspired by listening to instrumental music, and those who are influenced and inspired by listening to vocal music. I'd say that Ugo, Milton, Bob, Jack, and myself fall into the former category, and Jason and Roy into the latter. What do you think?

The International Whistle-Off

The IWO began in 1977, originally devised by a long-defunct computer company as a contest between human whistlers and the whistle sounds generated by their "technologically superior" computer. The computer and its parent company are long gone, while the IWO has prospered.

The subsequent dozen Whistle-Offs, sponsored by the Carson City, Nevada Chamber of Commerce, have become convocations of the world's finest whistlers, tourist attractions, and massive media events.

In 1989, the IAW purchased the rights

to sponsor the Whistle-Off. After a careful search, **John Ascuaga's Nugget** casino and hotel of Sparks (near Reno) Nevada was chosen to host the event. Mr. Ascuaga's energetic participation in the Whistle-Off promises to make this year's competition even more pleasurable and exciting for participants and spectators alike.

Dana and Bill Andrus of Chelsea Enterprises have handled the publicity for the event this year, and once again I'd like to thank them for their help in putting me in touch with the world's best whistlers!

The **American Lung Association of Nevada** (ALAN), with over 40 ongoing non-profit programs serving Nevada respiratory health needs, will be the beneficiary of this year's event. As Michael Melner, ALAN's president, stated: "The International Whistle-Off and ALAN have a natural pairing of interests, both being organizations that deal with breath."

National Whistlers Convention

The NWC is an offshoot of the Franklin County and Louisburg College Folk Festival. Founded in 1970 by **Allen de Hart**, Director of Public Affairs for the college, the festival showcased the traditional arts and crafts of the southeastern states. In 1974, Darrell Williams, of Durham, North Carolina, requested permission to whistle an original composition in the singing competition. The rest is history.

By 1980, the National Whistlers Convention had become a separate event, and today the NWC attracts contestants from nearly every state in the nation. The NWC has as much an educational component as a competitive one, featuring children's events, seminars and demonstrations by artists-in-residence throughout the spring weekend during which the Convention takes place.

Where To Go From Here

What else is there to do? Listen to lots of music, especially whistling music. Continue to study music theory. Learn to play an instrument or two (I can help you do that if you'd care to read my Sales Pitch), because learning a new instrument will give you lots of ideas and inspiration for your whistling. Join the International Association of Whistlers, and come to the International Whistle-Off and the National Whistlers Convention. And last but very far from least, whistle a lot, and enjoy it!

David's Harp Goodbye

Well, that's it for now, friends. I hope that you learned some, and that you enjoyed a lot. I sure learned plenty about whistlers and whistling from doing this book and recording, and I sincerely thank all you readers for giving me the opportunity to do so. If you like my harmonica "Outro" (it's the opposite of "Intro", I guess), be sure to read my offer on the next page!

Sales Pitch

The fact is that whistling is quite a bit harder than playing most other musical instruments. All the work takes place out of sight, and *you* are in charge of making sure you're on pitch. With harmonica, or guitar, you merely need to blow on the right reed, or put a finger on the right string, and you automatically get the note you need! So whistling is like driving a car with gearshift and clutch — a lot of physical technique is required. Other instruments are like driving with an automatic transmission — you only need worry about *where* you want to go (or, in my analogy, what you want to play).

Instant Blues Harmonica™, or, Zen & the Art of Blues Harp Blowing! covers mostly The Blues, with some folk and classical tunes. Like this package, it includes sections on the psychology of music and improvisation. We have over 4,000 fan letters on file for this 64 page book, 98 minute tape, and high quality harmonica. Our **kid's version** (for ages 4-9) is based on elements chosen from the effective Suzuki, Yamaha, and Orff-Schulwerk methods of music instruction. Each is only **$19.95** plus $2 postage & handling ($4 Canada, $6 foreign).

Or try our **Instant Flute™**! Our package will have you playing songs *within minutes*, and includes a 64 page book and a sweet-sounding, nickel-plated "block" style flute imported from England. **$14.95 for book and flute**, plus $2 postage & handling ($4 Canada, $6 foreign).

Whistle along with **Instant Guitar™** . The book and 98 minute cassette come with a ChordSnaffle™, my own invention. It allows even total beginners to play songs using just one finger (instead of three or four) to create chords instantly! Play simple folk, blues, classical, country, new age or jazz in just one hour! Hard to believe, but it works! **Complete for $14.95**, same p & h as others.

Open to something completely different, but unbelievably important? Then try **The Three Minute Meditator** (128 pp. $6.95 plus $2 p & h) and its sequel, **Metaphysical Fitness: The Complete 30 Day Plan for Your Mental, Emotional, and Spiritual Health** (240 pp. $7.95 plus $2.00 p & h). They're my first non-music books, based on many years study of matters metaphysical. In both of them, I apply the same type of step-by-step teaching methods that I've used in this book — to the subject of ... enlightenment!

As psychologist/author **Ram Dass** said of The Three Minute Meditator: "Had this book been available 25 years ago, it would've saved me a lot of trips (!) of all kinds!" The Three Minute Meditator has an exciting foreword by ice cream moguls **Ben & Jerry**. And, as they say, "If you think it's strange that a couple of guys who make ice cream for a living are writing a foreword for a book on meditation, then you probably shouldn't be reading a meditation book written by a harmonica player in the first place!"

We'd love to stay in contact with you, so if you'd like to be on our **mailing list**, drop us a line and include a stamped self-addressed envelope. We'll send you a copy of our **occasional newsletter!** And, if we get enough signs of interest, we might consider doing a sequel (perhaps on cassette) to this book. What do you think about that?